I0844460

The Effects of Economic Instability

An in-depth look at how a country's economic instability affects the lives of its individuals and the entire ecosystem.

By

Thompson Williams

Copyright © by Thompson Williams, 2023. All rights reserved.

The publisher's permission must be obtained before this work is replicated or reproduced in any way. As a result, the contents cannot be stored electronically, transferred, or stored in a database. The document cannot be copied, scanned, faxed, or saved in any form without the permission of the publisher or creator.

Table Of Contents

Conclusion

Introduction

The waves of instability in a country's economic landscape spread far beyond boardrooms and financial districts, casting a devastating shadow on the fundamental fabric of society. As the tides of economic uncertainty ebb and flow, the lives of its residents become inextricably linked with the unpredictability of fiscal instability. We dive into the visceral impact of economic insecurity on the everyday lives, aspirations, and well-being of individuals who navigate the turbulent waters of unpredictable economic climates in this narrative of financial complexities. Join us on a trip where the narrative is not confined to balance sheets but unfolds in the actual realities of residents, illustrating the subtle interplay between economic instability and human resilience.

Chapter 1
The Inflationary Ripple Effect

Economic insecurity frequently manifests itself as inflation, eroding citizens' purchasing power. This chapter investigates how rising prices affect individuals' daily lives, ranging from basic necessities to long-term financial planning.

The effects of rising prices on people's lives are as follows:

1. The Effect on Basic Needs

Rising prices put a real strain on people as the cost of basic necessities skyrockets. Grocery bills are increasing, making it difficult for families to maintain a balanced and nutritious diet. Food, toiletries, and utilities consume a larger portion of household budgets, leaving people with less discretionary income.

Access to healthcare can become a luxury as the rising cost of medical services and prescription medications strains people's finances. The repercussions extend to transportation, affecting commuters who face rising fuel and public transportation costs.

2. The Effect on Daily Expenses

Daily expenses like commuting, dining out, and recreational activities bear the brunt of inflation. Individuals are forced to reconsider and reduce discretionary spending, which has an impact on their quality of life. This financial strain may force people to make lifestyle changes and sacrifices as they prioritize essential needs over leisure and non-essential purchases.

3. The Effect on Savings and Investments

Long-term financial planning suffers as rising prices reduce the true value of savings and investments. Individuals preparing for major life events such as education, homeownership, or retirement must reevaluate their objectives. Inflation erodes the purchasing power of saved funds, necessitating a proactive approach to financial security.

4. Burden of Debt

Inflation can exacerbate the burden for those who are in debt. Loan repayments become more difficult as the value of money falls. Individuals may experience difficulties servicing loans, potentially resulting in increased debt stress and financial instability.

5. Concerns about employment and income

Economic insecurity, which is frequently linked to inflation, can lead to job insecurity and income fluctuations. Individuals may face unemployment or stagnant wages, exacerbating the difficulties of coping with rising prices. Anxiety caused by job insecurity pervades many aspects of people's lives, affecting not only their financial well-being but also their overall sense of security.

In essence, rising prices have an impact that goes beyond the immediate strain on purchasing power. It pervades many aspects of people's lives, influencing their daily decisions. Changing spending habits and requiring a reevaluation of long-term financial goals. Adaptability, financial literacy, and occasionally making difficult trade-offs are necessary to successfully navigate these challenges.

Chapter 2

Livelihoods and Unemployment

This chapter explores the difficulties that citizens encounter when job opportunities decrease, while also examining the direct correlation between economic instability and unemployment. It looks at how homes, mental health, and society as a whole are affected by domino effects.

1. Effect on Workplace Employment

There is more competition for available jobs when there are fewer job opportunities due to economic instability. Uncertainty about their professional prospects and unstable finances result from extended periods of unemployment experienced by job seekers. The difficulties people face navigating a contracting job market are covered in this segment.

- **A Rise in Rivals**

Job seekers compete more fiercely when the job market is contracting. Securing employment is more difficult because there is a larger pool of applicants than there are open positions. One of the biggest obstacles in a competitive job market is having to stand out.

- **Scarce Employment Opportunities**

People have fewer options for appropriate jobs when there are fewer job openings. As options become more limited, people may be forced to consider careers or industries outside of their first choices, which could result in a mismatch between skill sets and job requirements.

- **Fear of Unemployment**

Anxiety about unemployment is exacerbated by the uncertainty surrounding job availability. People's mental health and general well-being may be negatively impacted by stress and anxiety they feel about losing their current jobs or having difficulty finding new ones.

• Unchanging Salary and Benefits

When the labor market contracts, employers might gain the upper hand, which would mean flat pay and fewer benefits. Negotiating advantageous compensation packages may be difficult for some people. Causing a sense of job insecurity and financial strain.

• Backsets and Delays in Your Career

Career setbacks and delays may arise from the scarcity of job opportunities. Long-term career paths may be impacted by obstacles people encounter when trying to advance in their jobs, learn new skills, or take advantage of opportunities for professional growth.

• Insufficient work

Underemployment, or working in jobs that don't fully utilize one's skills and qualifications, is a common result of the job market's decline. Career advancement is hampered by this situation in addition to having an effect on job satisfaction.

• Unmatched Skills

The skills that people possess and the skills that employers are looking for may not match as a result of a shifting labor market. Due to this disparity, people may need to spend money on upskilling or retraining in order to successfully change jobs.

• Extended Job Search Times

People who are navigating a contracting job market frequently have to extend their job search times. Long-term job searches lead to monetary burdens, psychological tension, and a feeling of helplessness regarding the difficulties in finding work.

• Effects on the Work-Life Balance

Work-life balance can be impacted by the pressures of a contracting labor market. Longer workdays, more stress, and difficulties striking a healthy balance between work and personal life could result from the increased competition and job uncertainty.

● Instability in the Economy

A generalized feeling of financial insecurity is exacerbated by the contracting labor market. People might be concerned about their ability to meet their financial obligations, their stability in the financial system, and how difficulties in the job market will affect their overall financial well-being in the long run.

2. Stress in the Home

The lack of employment possibilities leads to greater financial strain on households, which sets off the domino effect at home. Reduced income can be a problem for families, making it harder to pay for necessities. Priorities become clear, and difficult choices may need adjusting one's lifestyle and causing tension in the family.

- **Priorities in Finance**

Financial priorities can cause lifestyle changes and strained family relationships. Making big lifestyle adjustments in order to prioritize needs over wants could lead to arguments within the family about how to divide up the available funds.

- **Switching Careers**

Career decisions can have an effect on family dynamics and way of life. Family members may experience stress or strain as a result of having to adjust to new routines due to changes in work schedules, job responsibilities, or even career paths.

- **Option for Education**

Lifestyle changes can result from decisions made regarding education, such as continuing education or choosing an alternative educational path. When family members balance the effects of educational decisions on time commitments and financial resources, tensions may arise.

- **Selecting a New Location**

Relocation decisions, whether for personal or professional reasons, can have a big influence on family dynamics and lifestyle. Especially if some family members disagree with the decision, adjusting to a new environment, school, and social circles can be stressful.

- **Priorities for Health and Wellbeing**

Lifestyle changes can result from placing a higher priority on choices related to health and wellness, such as changing to a healthier way of living or taking care of a medical condition. As family members adjust to changes in daily schedules, meal plans, caregiving responsibility and other factors, tensions may arise.

- **Prioritizing time management**

The way of life and the dynamics of the family can be affected by decisions made about time management priorities, such as how to balance work and personal life. Priorities may need to be discussed and schedule adjustments made for the family in order to strike the right balance.

- **Guidelines for Technology Use**

Making changes to one's lifestyle may result from setting rules about technology use in the family. A family's younger members who are accustomed to certain habits may become tense when boundaries are set regarding screen time or social media usage.

- **Investing Money**

Family dynamics and way of life can be impacted by decisions made regarding savings amounts and priorities. Conflict can result from divergent opinions about long-term financial objectives, investment strategies, and risk tolerance.

- **Selecting a Family Plan**

Making decisions about family planning, like how many kids to have or how far apart to put them, can drastically change one's lifestyle.

These choices could have an effect on family relationships, finances, and daily schedules.

- **Choosing to Own a Home**

Homeownership-related decisions, like purchasing a home or choosing to rent one, can cause changes in lifestyle and strain relationships within the family. Conflicts can arise from disparities in tastes or budgetary concerns.

- **Strategy for Retirement**

Decisions about retirement timelines and planning can have an impact on family dynamics and way of life. Disagreements and possible tensions may arise from changes in family roles, potential relocation, or adjustments to spending habits.

- **Family Spending Plans**

Lifestyle decisions can be influenced by decisions made regarding family finances and budgeting. Establishing stringent financial limits or making reductions could cause conflict within particularly if different opinions exist regarding the priorities of spending.

- **Business Initiatives**

Choosing to start a business or engage in entrepreneurial activities can cause changes in lifestyle and strain relationships within the family. Family dynamics may be strained by the time and money commitments that come with being an entrepreneur.

- **Charitable Priorities**

Choices about charitable contributions and philanthropic endeavors can influence one's way of life. Disagreements over priorities or values related to community involvement can spark conversations and possibly put strain on family relationships.

- **Aging and Care Decisions for the Elderly**

Decisions about assisted living or caregiving arrangements, for example, can have a big impact on how one lives as one ages and takes care of their elderly. Members of the family may experience tension as they work through the logistical and emotional ramifications of these choices.

3. Mental Health Repercussions

This chapter examines a crucial topic, the toll on mental health. Financial strains combined with the stress of unemployment can cause anxiety, depression, and a sense of hopelessness. Losing a job affects people's self-esteem and general well-being, going beyond just a financial hardship. This section looks into the coping strategies and psychological difficulties that people with limited employment experience.

A. Psychological Difficulties

- **Fear of Job Insecurity**

People who are unemployed frequently suffer from anxiety because they are unsure of their job situation. An ongoing source of stress and emotional strain can result from the fear of losing one's job or from not being able to find one.

- **Financial Stress**

Numerous psychological issues are exacerbated by the financial strain brought on by a lack of employment. Feelings of inadequacy, frustration, and helplessness are common as people struggle to meet their financial obligations on a limited income.

- **Self-Esteem and Identity Concerns**

People's self-esteem and sense of identity can be negatively impacted by job scarcity, particularly if they strongly identify with their professional roles. A job loss or inability to find employment can result in feelings of worthlessness and identity crisis.

- **Social Comparison and Stigma**

People compare their professional status to others when faced with job scarcity. The stigmatized employment policies of unemployment or underemployment can exacerbate feelings of shame and isolation.

• Career Setbacks and Dissatisfaction

Having difficulty finding the jobs you want to do can make you feel frustrated and like you've failed in your career. People may struggle with unfulfilled career goals, unfulfilled expectations, and uncertainty about their future professional paths.

B. Coping Techniques

• Social support and networking

Creating and utilizing professional networks and asking friends and family for assistance can act as an important psychological safety net. During trying times, social ties provide a feeling of community, networking opportunities, and emotional support.

• The Acquisition of Skills and Ongoing Education

Continuous learning and skill development are coping mechanisms as well as ways to improve employability. It instills a proactive mentality and gives people a sense of control over their professional development.

- **Techniques for Stress Reduction and Mindfulness**

In the face of job scarcity, adopting mindfulness practices and stress-reduction strategies like deep breathing exercises or meditation can help people manage their anxiety and retain mental health.

- **Flexibility and Adaptability**

One coping strategy is to practice flexibility and adaptability in one's expectations and goals for one's career. People who are flexible and open to new ideas may have an easier time adjusting to the shortage of jobs.

- **Having Reasonable Expectations and Goals**

People can better control their expectations and lessen the psychological effects of unfulfilled career aspirations by setting realistic short- and long-term goals. This strategy encourages pride in accomplishment, even for minor victories.

- **Consulting a Professional**

Seeking advice and assistance from mentors, coaches, or career counselors can be very beneficial. Professionals working in these capacities can help people with psychological issues, improving job search tactics, and investigating new career avenues.

- **Sustaining a Harmonious Work-Life Balance**

It is essential to stress the value of preserving a positive work-life balance. Hobbies, physical activity, and social connections are examples of extracurricular activities that enhance general wellbeing and resilience in trying times.

- **Positive Thoughts and Mentality Modifications**

Reframing perspectives can be facilitated by adopting positive affirmations and mindset shifts. Despite the difficulties of job scarcity, putting an emphasis on one's strengths, accomplishments, and personal development promotes a more optimistic outlook.

- **Contribution and Involvement in the Community**

By giving back to the community and creating a sense of purpose, volunteering or participating in community activities can help people overcome the detrimental psychological effects of job scarcity by fostering social connections and a positive sense of contribution to society.

- **Remedial Measures**

A safe space to examine and treat psychological issues related to job scarcity can be provided by seeking professional therapeutic interventions, such as counseling or therapy.

Emotional stability and coping mechanisms can be obtained with professional help.

4. The State of Society

It looks at how declining employment prospects affect society welfare through a more comprehensive lens. Social unrest brought on by higher unemployment rates can undermine community cohesion. This section explores how people may deal with the fallout from this, and how it might affect public health, crime rates, and the general fabric of society.

A. Rates of Crime

• Rise in Crimes Against Property

Reduced work prospects could result in a rise in property crimes like burglaries and thefts since people in need of money might turn to illegal ways to get by.

• Economically Driven Offenses

As people look for other sources of income, economic desperation can lead to an increase in economically motivated crimes, such as fraud, embezzlement, and white-collar crimes.

- **Youth Involvement in Crimes**

Young people who have difficulty finding work may become more involved in criminal activity as a result of limited employment opportunities, which can disproportionately affect younger people.

B. Public Health

- **Issues in Mental Health**

People's levels of stress, anxiety, and depression are frequently increased by economic uncertainty and a lack of jobs. Stress on mental health can have a significant impact on general well-being and possibly contribute to a rise in mental health problems, which can have broad implications for public health.

- **Healthcare Accessible**

Affected people may have less access to healthcare as a result of diminished employment opportunities. People without insurance or with inadequate insurance may put off getting treatment, which can worsen existing conditions and put a strain on the healthcare system.

- **Alcohol Abuse**

A contributing factor to rising rates of substance abuse is economic distress. When people experience financial hardships or unemployment, they may use drugs as a coping strategy, which raises questions about addiction and related public health issues.

C. The Social Fabric and Community Well-Being

- **Pressure on Social Cohesion**

Economic insecurity can put a strain on community social cohesion. Increased financial stress and competition for limited resources may promote individualism rather than community collaboration, affecting the social fabric as a whole.

- **Unrest in the Community**

Reduced job opportunities may cause community unrest and dissatisfaction. As a result of economic disparities, protests, demonstrations, and social movements may emerge, contributing to social and political tensions.

- **The Effect on Education**

Families facing financial difficulties may find it difficult to invest in education, potentially resulting in lower educational attainment and limiting opportunities for future generations. This can have long-term consequences for affected communities' social mobility.

D. Family Relations

- **Enhanced Stress in Families**

Lack of work can exacerbate family stress, strain relationships, and even cause family dynamics to break down. Financial strains can exacerbate disputes and have an adverse effect on families' general well-being.

- **Effects on Youngsters**

The wellbeing of children living in impacted households may be impacted by limited employment opportunities. Financial difficulties can make it difficult for families to give their kids the resources, support, and education they need, which can have an impact on their long-term results.

E. Administration and Social Services

- **Stress on the Social Sector**

Economic hardships and rising unemployment put more pressure on government assistance programs and social services. Stretched

31

government resources could affect how well safety nets and support systems work.

• **Possibility of Policy Adjustments**

Government interventions and policy changes may result from the societal repercussions of reduced employment opportunities. To address the wider societal ramifications, governments may need to reevaluate their employment plans, social policies, and economic recovery initiatives.

5. Long-Term Effects and Skill Erosion

Understanding the long-term effects of limited job opportunities centers on the erosion of skills and professional stagnation. People might lose employable skills, which would make it more difficult for them to rejoin the workforce when opportunities do eventually present themselves. During times of job scarcity, the chapter discusses upskilling, skill retention, and the value of ongoing professional development.

- **Constant Learning Attitude**

Developing an attitude of perpetual learning is crucial when employment is scarce. Adopting the mindset that learning is a continuous process inspires people to become more inquisitive, flexible, and proactive in their pursuit of new knowledge.

- **Electronic Learning and Online Courses**

Upskilling opportunities are easily and conveniently accessible when using e-learning platforms and online courses. With the convenience of home, people can learn new skills through platforms such as Coursera, Udacity, and LinkedIn Learning, which provide a vast array of courses.

- **Certifications Related to Industry**

A person's professional credentials are improved and their dedication to staying current in a particular field is demonstrated by obtaining certifications that are pertinent to the industry. By demonstrating their expertise to prospective employers, certifications can increase an individual's competitiveness in the job market.

- **Networking and Professional Associations**

Participating in professional associations and networking with colleagues in the industry offers helpful insights into new trends and skill requirements. Attend workshops, webinars, and conferences to stay up to date on industry advancements and broaden your professional network.

- **Cross-Functional Training**

Seeking out opportunities for cross-functional training enables people to diversify their skill set. Knowing how to apply skills from one industry or role to another promotes resilience and adaptability, which increases one's marketability.

- **Mentorship and Guidance**

Seeking out mentorship and guidance from seasoned industry professionals offers insightful information about skill requirements and career strategies.

- **Learning through Projects**

Applying theoretical knowledge in real-world contexts is made possible by project-based learning. Taking on projects, either alone or with others, gives you practical experience and demonstrates how you can use the skills you've learned.

- **Participate in Industry Conferences and Webinars**

One can stay up to date on the newest advancements and trends by actively participating in industry webinars, conferences, and seminars. Experts who discuss the future direction of the industry and skill requirements are frequently featured at these events.

- **Build Soft Skills**

Soft skills like problem-solving, communication, and flexibility are just as vital as technical skills. Professional success and employability are increased when an emphasis is placed on building a well-rounded skill set.

- **Employ Corporate Training Initiatives**

Utilizing the training programs provided by the current employer is a wise move if you are employed. Participating in these programs can improve current skills and help advance a career, as many companies invest in employee development.

- **Industry Study and Analysis of Trends**

Those who regularly conduct trend analysis and industry research are better able to keep up with the constantly changing skill requirements.

Knowing the industry's needs both now and in the future helps people identify areas for skill development in a proactive manner.

- **Peer Education and Cooperative Initiatives**

A collaborative learning environment is promoted by working together on projects with peers or taking part in group learning exercises. Through knowledge sharing and idea exchange, peer learning enables people to improve their skill sets as a group.

- **Keep Up With New Developments in Technology**

It's essential to stay up to date on new developments in the field of technology. Rapid technological change presents opportunities for people to position themselves as important contributors in their fields.

6. Policies of the Government and Social Safety Nets

Examined is the function of social safety nets and government regulations in easing the difficulties brought on by a decline in employment prospects. This covers talks about retraining programs, unemployment insurance, and programs designed to help people and families during recessions.

- **Unemployment Insurance**

Governments have the power to create and expand programs for unemployment benefits, which give people who lose their jobs financial support. These benefits serve as an essential safety net, providing a short-term source of income while people look for other work opportunities.

- **Initiatives for Reskilling and Job Training**

By putting job training and reskilling initiatives into practice, people can learn new skills that are in line with changing market demands. Governments can work with companies and academic institutions to offer training programs that improve employability in developing fields.

- **Packages of Economic Stimulus**

Governments can use economic stimulus packages to reinvest funds into the economy when job opportunities are scarce. These packages, which seek to boost economic growth and generate new job opportunities, may include tax breaks, subsidies, and infrastructure projects.

- **Assistance for Medium-Sized and Small Businesses (SMEs)**

Supporting SMEs with grants, capital, and advantageous laws and regulations contributes to the preservation and growth of employment. SMEs frequently make major contributions to employment, and with the right assistance, they can overcome financial difficulties and keep their staff.

- **Rules and Policies for the Workplace**

Governments have a part to play in creating and implementing workplace rules and guidelines that support job security. Anti-discrimination laws, fair labor practices, and layoff regulations all help to create a more secure and stable work environment for employees.

- **Social Safety Nets for Groups at Risk**

It is essential to strengthen social safety nets for vulnerable groups, such as low-income people, single parents, and people with disabilities. Programs for targeted assistance, like food and housing subsidies, lessen the negative effects of job scarcity on the most vulnerable members of society.

- **Placement Services for Jobs**

Job placement services funded by the government help people locate new employment opportunities. These services can include career counseling, job fairs, and online job-seeker-employer platforms, enabling a more effective and efficient approach to finding a job.

- **Programs for Temporary Employment**

During recessions, businesses can retain workers by implementing temporary employment schemes like work-sharing or subsidized employment. These programs protect jobs while offering financial support to businesses.

- **Programs for Public Works**

Public works initiatives are a tool that governments can use to address unemployment and infrastructure development. These initiatives support community development and economic recovery by generating employment opportunities in the maintenance, construction, and other sectors.

- **Mental Health Support and Accessible Healthcare**

When jobs are scarce, it is imperative to guarantee that people have access to affordable healthcare. People can address health issues and manage the psychological difficulties brought on by unemployment with the support of government policies that facilitate access to mental health and healthcare services.

• Assistance for Training and Education

Encouraging people to invest in their professional development is achieved through providing subsidies for education and training programs. The workforce's skill sets are improved through government support of educational opportunities, increasing their competitiveness in the labor market.

• Protections from Redundancy

Employers are better protected during layoffs when redundancy protections are enforced through legal frameworks. Regulations requiring employers to give workers affected by job loss fair compensation, notice periods, or support services can be established by governments.

Basically, this chapter shows the various difficulties people encounter when their employment options are limited. It emphasizes the need for comprehensive approaches to address the complex web of issues arising from a scarcity of employment opportunities, acknowledging the far-reaching consequences on households, mental health, and societal well-being.

Chapter 3

Social Services and Austerity Measures

Austerity measures are imposed by governments in response to economic turmoil, which has an impact on social services. This chapter looks into how citizens' struggles are made worse by limited access to healthcare, education, and other necessities.

A. Effect on Access to Healthcare

This section explores the concrete effects of economic instability on the availability of healthcare for citizens. People may find it increasingly difficult to pay for necessary medical care and prescription drugs as their financial difficulties worsen. The story highlights the possible long-term repercussions of delaying or forgoing medical care as it examines the challenging decisions people must make when weighing their health needs against financial constraints.

- **Affordability Difficulties**

Many citizens may find it more difficult to afford healthcare services as a result of economic instability, which can lower household incomes. High initial out-of-pocket costs, medical treatments may be delayed or foregone as a result of limited financial resources, negatively impacting an individual's health outcomes.

- **Unemployment and Health Insurance Loss**

Economic downturns are frequently accompanied by higher unemployment rates. Job loss can lead to the loss of employer-sponsored health insurance, leaving people without adequate coverage. Because of cost concerns, people may be discouraged from seeking necessary medical care.

- **Medication Availability Is Limited**

Affordability issues can extend to medications, with citizens having difficulty purchasing prescribed medications. Individuals may resort to rationing medications or avoiding necessary prescriptions in some cases, resulting in worsened health conditions and increased healthcare complications.

- **Public Healthcare Systems Under Stress**

As more people rely on government-funded healthcare services because they lack private insurance, economic instability may put a pressure on public healthcare systems. Budgetary restrictions combined with rising demand may lead to longer wait times, worse care, and restricted access to specialized treatments.

- **Effect on Healthcare Prevention**

People may be deterred from investing in preventive healthcare practices like regular check-ups and screenings by uncertain economic times. Prioritizing short-term financial concerns over preventive care can raise the risk of health problems going unnoticed and result in more expensive long-term treatments.

- **Behavioral Health Issues**

Stress and anxiety levels are frequently higher when there is economic instability. The effect on mental health may cause new mental health problems to arise or worsen pre-existing ones. The general state of well-being may be further impacted by restricted access to mental health services.

- **Postponed or Abandoned Medical Operations**

Individuals who are struggling financially may decide to put off or forego elective medical procedures. When people eventually seek medical attention, this delay may cause health conditions to worsen and require more involved and expensive treatments.

- **Healthcare Workforce Reduction**

Budget cuts in the healthcare industry could result from unstable economic conditions, which would impact staffing and resource levels. Longer wait times, a decline in the quality of care, and a reduction in the number of healthcare professionals available are all possible outcomes of workforce reductions.

- **Influence on Populations at Risk**

Uncertainty in the economy disproportionately affects vulnerable groups, such as the poor and marginalized communities. Health disparities are made worse by a lack of resources, including money and access to healthcare, which leads to differences in health results.

- **Reduction in Infrastructure Investment for Healthcare**

The capacity of healthcare facilities may be limited as a result of governments cutting back on infrastructure investments due to economic instability. This may lead to challenges in effectively responding to public health emergencies, overcrowding in hospitals, and a lack of medical equipment.

- **Coverage Vagaries for Health Insurance**

In particular, for people in temporary jobs or independent contractors, economic downturns may result in gaps in health insurance coverage. Individuals with coverage gaps may forego essential medical care or incur high costs for care.

B. Obstacles in Education

The chapter goes into more detail on how access to education is hampered by economic instability. Families that are struggling financially might find it difficult to pay for educational supplies like technology, books, and school fees. This section examines the emerging educational disparities that impact children's academic achievement and prospects in the future.

Among the ways that financial instability restricts access to education are

- **Barriers to Affordability**

Unpredictability in the economy can cause financial hardships for both individuals and families, making it challenging to pay for educational expenses. This covers books, transportation, tuition, and other associated costs. Access to both primary and higher education may be restricted by financial obstacles.

- **Fall in Funding for Education**

Government budgetary constraints during times of economic instability may result in a reduction in funding for education. Access to high-quality education may be hampered by this decrease in funding, which may also lead to program cuts, fewer resources for schools, and restrictions on scholarship opportunities.

• Higher Dropout Rates

Increased dropout rates at different educational levels can be attributed to economic instability. Family financial strains may compel students to drop out of school early in order to support the family or take advantage of job opportunities, which will impede their academic progress.

• Restricted Technological Access

Although there is a growing trend toward technology-enhanced learning, access to necessary devices and internet connectivity may be hindered by economic instability. There may be inequalities in educational opportunities if students lack access to technology and find it difficult to participate in online learning.

• Decreased Assistance for Educational Establishments

Economic downturns may cause educational institutions to receive less funding, which will have an effect on the caliber of education they are able to offer. This might result in inadequate infrastructure, out-of-date resources, and understaffing, which would hinder effective learning.

- **Difficulties in Paying for Higher Education**

Access to higher education may be particularly impacted by economic instability. Many people may find it financially unfeasible to pursue a college or university education due to rising tuition costs and dwindling financial aid options, which may limit their career prospects.

- **Effects on the Infrastructure of Education**

Economic difficulties may make it more difficult to invest in educational infrastructure, which could have an impact on the physical state of colleges and universities. Inadequate classrooms, outdated infrastructure, and a dearth of contemporary amenities can all contribute to a bad learning environment.

- **Errors in the Course of Education**

Disruptions in educational programs can result from economic instability. This could affect the whole educational experience by limiting the availability of enrichment programs, cutting back on extracurricular activities, and reducing access to educational support services.

- **Insufficient Number of Teaching Staff**

Job freezes and layoffs in the education sector are possible outcomes of economic downturns. Reduced individual attention, larger class sizes, and a general deterioration in educational quality can result from a shortage of qualified teachers and other educational personnel.

- **Higher Student Loan Amounts**

Student loan decisions to finance their education can be influenced by unstable economies. Student loan debt can have a long-term negative impact on people's financial security and capacity to make other investments, like buying a house, as well as business.

- **Restricted Utilization of Learning Materials**

The availability of vital educational resources like textbooks, study guides, and instructional technology may be restricted by unstable economic conditions. Gaining access to the tools required for successful learning may be difficult for students from economically disadvantaged homes.

- **Repercussions for vocational and specialized training**

Programs for vocational and specialized training may become less accessible due to economic volatility. Some industries may have fewer resources and training options available to people seeking skills for those industries, which could limit their ability to enter or advance in those fields.

Following are some examples of the educational disparities that arise and impact children's academic development and future opportunities:

- **Gaps in the availability of high-quality education**

Unequal access to high-quality education is frequently a result of economic instability. Well-equipped schools may not be readily available to children in economically disadvantaged areas.

- **Unfair Technology Access**

Education disparities may worsen as a result of the shift to technology-enhanced learning. Limited access to computers, the internet, and other digital tools may make it difficult for students to keep up with online learning, which could have an adverse effect on their academic performance and future prospects.

- **Elementary Childhood Education Inequalities**

Programs for early childhood education may become less accessible due to economic instability. The lack of access to high-quality preschool or daycare for children from economically disadvantaged families may affect their development of foundational skills and preparedness for formal education.

- **Diverse Opportunities Outside of School**

Financial difficulties might restrict the extracurricular activities that students can participate in. Rich schools frequently provide more extracurricular activities, like leadership courses, sports, and the arts, giving students a wider range of skills and improving their overall development.

- **Effects on Services for Special Education**

Reduced funding and services for special education could be the outcome of unstable economic conditions. Students with special needs are disproportionately affected by this, as it restricts their access to support and accommodations that they require. This can have an adverse effect on their academic performance and future opportunities.

- **Inequitable Entry into Honors and Advanced Placement (AP) Courses**

There might be fewer honors and advanced placement (AP) courses offered by high schools in economically underprivileged areas. This inequality restricts students' chances to push themselves academically and could have an impact on their admissions to specific universities and career pathways.

- **Restricted Services for College Counseling**

The availability of college counseling services in schools may be impacted by financial difficulties. Rich schools might have more resources available to help students with their college careers, such as help with applications and scholarships, giving their pupils a leg up when they pursue higher education.

- ### **Effects on Student-Teacher Ratios and Teacher Quality**

In schools with limited resources, economic instability may result in teacher layoffs and larger class sizes. Increased student-teacher ratios and a shortage of qualified teachers could lower the standard of instruction and have an impact on students' future prospects and academic performance.

- ### **Differences in the Preparation of Standardized Tests**

Students from low-income families might not have as much access to tutoring or test-prep courses as other students do to resources for preparing for standardized exams. This may affect how well they score on standardized tests, which may have an effect on their chances of getting into college and receiving scholarships.

- **Inequitable Access to Career Counseling**

Services for career guidance may not always be available due to financial difficulties. Richer students might have greater access to internships, mentorships, and exposurc to a range of professional pathways, giving them a more defined course for the future.

- **Influence on Options for Post-Secondary Education**

Choices about post-secondary education can be influenced by economic instability. Financially strapped students might choose less expensive options, which would prevent them from enrolling in specialized programs or attending prestigious universities that might improve their chances of landing a good job later on.

- **Parental Involvement Effects**

Parental involvement in schooling may be impacted by economic difficulties. Financially unstable parents might not have the time or resources to fully participate in their kids' education, which could have an impact on academic support and involvement in extracurricular activities.

C. Social Services Erosion

Beyond healthcare and education, other essential services are also examined. Budget cuts are a common result of economic downturns, which have an effect on the accessibility and caliber of public services.The social safety nets that residents depend on most during hard times are diminished, from public transit to social services. This section highlights how vulnerable populations are disproportionately impacted by reduced social services and the societal ramifications that follow.

- **Effect on Access to Healthcare**

For vulnerable populations, fewer social services can mean less access to healthcare. This exacerbates health disparities and jeopardizes general well-being by limiting access to medical care, mental health services, and preventive care.

- **A Rise in Economic Inequalities**

Cuts to social services disproportionately affect vulnerable populations that are already struggling financially. Reductions in food assistance, housing support, and welfare programs widen the gap between various socioeconomic groups and increase economic inequality.

- **Homelessness and Insecurity of Housing**

Reduced social services can put vulnerable populations at risk of homelessness and unstable housing. The lack of stable living conditions for individuals and families resulting from cuts to housing assistance programs, shelters, and affordable housing initiatives exacerbates societal problems.

- **Pressure on Social Media Platforms**

Frequently, vulnerable groups depend on community organizations and social support networks for aid. Reduced social services put more strain on these networks and make it harder for them to help people in need by offering vital resources, guidance, and support.

- **Curriculum Inequalities**

Education disparities can be caused by cuts to social services, especially for children who are more vulnerable. Students from disadvantaged backgrounds are disproportionately affected by reduced school funding, restricted access to educational support programs, and insufficient resources, which impedes their academic progress.

- **Higher Rates of Crime**

Reduced social services, particularly in communities that are already vulnerable, may be a factor in rising crime rates. When people experience financial hardships and lack of access to job and educational opportunities, their options become more limited, which can contribute to an increase in criminal activity.

- **Mental Health Issues**

When social services are cut, vulnerable populations may face more severe mental health issues. A person's general well-being is further impacted by stress, anxiety, and depression when they lack access to counseling, thcrapy, and other mental health resources.

- **Having Problems with Substance Abuse**

Reductions in social services may exacerbate the vulnerable population's struggles with substance abuse. Substance abuse problems may worsen if rehabilitation centers, addiction treatment programs, and mental health services are inaccessible.

- **Effects on Young People and Children**

Reduced social services have a particularly negative impact on vulnerable children and young people. Cuts to after-school programs, youth services, and child welfare programs may deprive these people of vital support networks, which could have detrimental long-term effects.

• Stress on Charity Establishments

When social services are scarce, non-profit organizations that frequently fill the gaps may experience a rise in demand and a fall in resources. The ability of these organizations to support vulnerable populations may be hampered by this strain.

• Decreased Legal Assistance Access

When social services are cut, vulnerable populations might have trouble getting legal aid. Legal aid programs may be overburdened or have limited resources available to assist people with housing, employment, and family-related legal issues.

• Effects of the Aging Population

The elderly population is particularly vulnerable to reduced social services. Seniors may become more isolated, experience health issues, and have a lower quality of life as a result of cuts to community support programs, healthcare services, and senior assistance programs.

D. Insecurity in Housing

The chapter shifts its emphasis to the housing industry and looks at the relationship between housing insecurity and economic instability. Keeping up stable housing becomes an enormous challenge as people battle with losing their jobs and experiencing financial instability. Examining the connection between evictions, homelessness, and economic downturns, the conversation highlights the profound effects on people as well as communities.

- **Financial instability and job loss**

Financial instability and a large loss of jobs are frequent outcomes of economic downturns. Losing their jobs can make it difficult for someone to pay their rent or mortgage, enhancing the likelihood of homelessness and eviction.

- **Home Market Instability and Foreclosures**

A wave of foreclosures can be set off by economic downturns, which also add to the instability of the housing market. Financially struggling homeowners run the risk of losing their houses, which adds to the general rise in housing insecurity.

- **Displacement and Evictions**

Landlords may have trouble collecting rental payments as the economy deteriorates. This may lead to evictions, which drive people and families from their houses and into a cycle of displaced living that frequently ends in homelessness.

- **Effect on Hiring Markets**

Unbalances in rental markets can result from economic downturns. Renters may have more difficulties because of landlords who take advantage of the increased demand for affordable housing, while some landlords may struggle to maintain their properties due to financial limitations.

• Inadequate Accessible Housing

A scarcity of reasonably priced housing options may be exacerbated by economic downturns. There are few options for individuals and families when it comes to finding affordable rental properties due to the confluence of unstable housing markets and job losses.

• Demand on Homeless Services and Shelters

Support services and shelters for the homeless are severely strained by the rise in evictions and homelessness. The increasing demand for emergency housing, food, and support for individuals facing homelessness is frequently too much for these organizations to handle.

• Effects on Emotional State

A decline in the economy can lead to homelessness and evictions, which can have a serious negative impact on mental health.

Anxiety and depression are more common in those impacted by homelessness due to stress related to losing one's house, uncertainty about the future, and difficulties navigating homelessness.

- **Interruptions in the Field of Education**

Education will be disrupted for children and youth who are homeless as a result of economic downturns. Their academic performance is impacted by frequent changes in living arrangements and restricted access to resources, which has long-term implications for their prospects in the future.

- **The Poverty Cycle**

Homelessness and evictions are factors in the poverty cycle. It can be challenging for people and families facing housing instability to obtain steady employment, access education, and overcome the obstacles brought on by financial hardship.

- **Restricted Community Assets**

Community resources are strained as a result of an increase in evictions and homelessness. Due to increased demands, social services, nonprofits, and local governments may find it difficult to give those in need the help they require.

- **Issues with Public Health**

Public health is at risk when economic downturns lead to homelessness. Health disparities among homeless populations can be made worse by inadequate living conditions, poor sanitation, and limited access to healthcare and sanitation services.

- **Community Welfare and Social Cohesion**

Community social cohesion may be impacted by the rise in homelessness. An increase in visible homelessness can cause interpersonal conflicts, strain community ties, and make it more difficult to promote the sense of wellbeing of both housed and homeless people.

E. Community Welfare

The general well-being of the communities impacted by fewer access points to necessary services is examined from a wider angle. The relationship between social cohesiveness and economic instability is examined in this section, along with how the strain on social services, healthcare, and education adds to community tension and the possibility of unrest.

- **Public health concerns and the strain on healthcare**

Uncertainty in the economy can put a burden on healthcare systems and restrict access to necessary services. Increased demand from the economically disadvantaged and decreased financing and resources for healthcare all contribute to public health issues, which in turn increase stress and discontent in the community.

- **Education Inequalities and Prospects for the Future**

Education disparities are frequently caused by economic instability. Inequality is exacerbated by a lack of funding for schools, restricted access to extracurricular activities, and difficulties in delivering high-quality instruction. This may cause dissatisfaction, especially in young people, which could harm community harmony.

- **Reduction of Social Services and Vulnerable Populations**

Vulnerable populations are disproportionately affected by cuts to social services. A decrease in funding for community programs, housing aid, and mental health services exacerbates stress in the most vulnerable, exacerbating social inequality and possibly inciting unrest.

- **Stress on Local Resources**

Social support networks and community resources are strained by economic instability. Increased demands for assistance may be difficult for nonprofits, community centers, and local agencies to handle, which could leave the community feeling frustrated and inadequate.

- **Unemployment and Precarious Employment**

Increased unemployment and job insecurity are frequently caused by economic instability. The ensuing financial burden on people and families weakens the sense of economic security and well-being in the community and adds to community stress.

- **Unrest in the Community and Housing Insecurity**

Unrest in a community can be exacerbated by housing instability brought on by financial difficulties. The general cohesion of neighborhoods and communities is impacted by the sense of instability that is brought about by evictions, homelessness, and housing insecurity.

- **Unequal Access to Opportunities**

Inequalities in opportunity are a result of economic instability. Inequality is perceived as existing within the community due to a lack of social services, educational opportunities, and employment opportunities, which can lead to tension and possible unrest.

- **Social Dynamics and Mental Health Issues**

Community social dynamics are impacted by the economic downturn's negative effects on mental health, which are made worse by limited access to mental health services. Relationship tension brought on by elevated stress, anxiety, and depression can exacerbate communal unease.

- **Unhappiness Among Youth and Their Prospects**

The future outlook is impacted by economic instability, especially for young people. Social unrest and protests may result from a lack of educational opportunities and worries about job prospects, which fuel dissatisfaction and frustration.

- **The Way the Community Views the Government's Response**

The way the government handles economic hardships is a major factor in maintaining community harmony. Community tension can be increased and public institution trust can be undermined by perceived shortcomings or disparities in government interventions.

- **Challenges Facing Small Enterprises and the Local Economy**

The local economy and small businesses are impacted by economic instability. Local business conflicts add to the stress felt by the community as residents see their neighborhood's economies deteriorate and fear for the future of locally owned businesses.

- **Effects on Mutual Trust**

Within a community, social trust can be undermined by economic instability. A decrease in trust among community members can have a negative effect on social cohesion and cooperative efforts. This can be caused by worries about job security, access to healthcare, and general well-being.

F. New Ideas and Community-Based Solutions

The chapter also features examples of grassroots projects and inventiveness that arise in reaction to restricted access to basic services. Resilience and resourcefulness are demonstrated when communities band together to fill the voids left by overburdened public services. The importance of community-driven solutions in easing the hardships brought on by economic instability is emphasized in this section.

- **Community-Based Empowerment**

Individuals are empowered at the local level by community-driven solutions. Communities can work together to address the particular problems brought on by economic instability by including locals in decision-making processes, which promotes a sense of agency and ownership.

- **Personalized Interventions**

Interventions that are customized to the unique needs and dynamics of the community are made possible by community-driven solutions. With the help of local knowledge, specific solutions to the most urgent problems locals encounter during hard times financially can be identified.

- **Networks of Social Assistance**

Social support networks are reinforced by community-driven approaches. In order to overcome the obstacles brought on by economic instability, locals can establish networks that share resources, offer emotional support, and cooperate by fostering cooperation and collaboration.

- **Strengthening   Resilience Neighborhoods**

Resilience can be strengthened through community-driven solutions. Involving locals in the conception and execution of projects improves community cohesion and makes it easier for them to bounce back from financial losses.

- **Acquiring and Exchanging Knowledge**

Knowledge exchange and skill development initiatives are facilitated by local solutions. To help citizens develop their skills and become better prepared to face economic uncertainty and pursue their goals, communities can host training sessions, workshops, and mentorship programs.

- **Boosting Regional Markets**

Supporting regional companies and economies is a common goal of community-driven solutions. Self-sufficiency is fostered at the community level by initiatives that support entrepreneurship, local commerce, and job creation.

- **Unity and Inclusion in Society**

Community-driven solutions improve inclusion and social cohesion. These methods assist in closing social gaps, advancing equity, and guaranteeing that everyone can benefit from community projects by including a variety of voices in the decision-making process.

- **Gathering Resources**

Local resources can be mobilized through community-driven initiatives. Community members can combine their resources to establish a safety net that lessens the effects of economic instability on vulnerable individuals and families, whether through volunteerism, fundraising, or shared services.

- **Collaboration and Advocacy**

Solutions that are pushed by the community encourage advocacy and group effort. Together, locals can make a greater impact on reducing financial hardships by pushing for enhanced social services, better legislation, and more backing from outside organizations.

- **Promoting Innovation**

Methods centered around community involvement promote creativity. The community is encouraged to be innovative because locals have a tendency to have distinct perspectives on the problems they encounter and can come up with original solutions that may not be obvious to higher echelons of government.

- **Enduring Progress**

Innovative community-based approaches support long-term growth. Through an eye toward the community's long-term health, citizens can put policies into place that support social cohesion, economic stability, and environmental sustainability.

- **Establishing Civic Engagement and Trust**

Trust and civic engagement are increased by community-driven solutions. There are more sustainable and practical solutions when community members actively shape the future of their neighborhood. This is because it increases their sense of civic responsibility and commitment.

In conclusion, this chapter examines the complex issues that arise for citizens when the state of the economy causes them to have less access to vital services like healthcare and education. It highlights the need for comprehensive approaches to address the vulnerabilities that arise during periods of economic uncertainty and examines the complex web of hardships, ranging from individual health decisions to wider societal consequences.

Chapter4
Worldwide Effects of Currency Depreciation

This chapter investigates the volatility of a nation's currency in the global marketplace. The effect is felt by the public in terms of their capacity to trade and participate in international markets, which affects both personal and governmental economic success.

1. Exchange Rate Variations and International Trade

The complex dynamics of how a nation's currency fluctuation reverberates on the global stage are explored in this chapter. It looks at how a weaker currency can make a nation more export-oriented while making imports more difficult, and how that affects international trade. It clarifies the intricate balance that affects trade balances and exchange rates, which in turn affects international economic relations.

- **Exchange Rates and the Competitiveness of Exports**

An important factor in assessing a nation's export competitiveness is its exchange rate. A country's exports may increase and its economy may generally improve if its goods and services are more reasonably priced for overseas consumers due to a weaker home currency.

- **Imbalances in Trade and Import Costs**

Exchange rate fluctuations affect how much imports cost. A country's trade imbalances may result from higher import costs brought on by a declining domestic currency because it forces the country to pay more for goods and services from abroad.

- **Effect on Trade Deficit or Surplus**

Changes in exchange rates can influence whether a nation has a trade surplus or deficit. Because imports are comparatively more expensive and exports are more competitive, a weaker currency generally improves the trade balance and may even result in a surplus.

- **Appreciation of Currency and Import-Driven Growth**

However, a strengthening national currency may promote growth driven by imports. A stronger currency helps consumers by lowering the cost of imports, but it can also encourage more imports, which could increase the trade deficit.

- **Exchange Rate Regulations and Market Competition**

A nation's ability to compete in international trade may be impacted by exchange rate-related government policies. Certain countries may implement measures to deliberately devalue or appreciate their currencies in order to improve their export standing or manage inflation.

- **International Supply Chains and Exchange Rates**

Exchange rate fluctuations have a significant impact on global supply chains. Exchange rate fluctuations affect the price of foreign-sourced inputs and components, which in turn affects how competitively priced finished goods are on the world market.

- **Trade Equilibrium and Financial Stability**

Both surpluses and deficits in trade that persist over time can have an impact on a country's economic stability. Long-term surpluses can produce foreign exchange reserves, while long-term deficits can result in the build-up of external debt, both of which have an impact on economic stability.

- **Exchange Rate Unpredictability and Business Scheduling**

For companies that trade internationally, high exchange rate volatility creates uncertainty. For importers and exporters, sudden and erratic changes in exchange rates can have a negative impact on profit margins and complicate long-term business planning.

- **Interventions by Central Banks**

To stabilize exchange rates or accomplish particular economic goals, central banks may intervene in the currency market. Trade balances can be affected by interventions that change the value of the national currency in relation to other currencies.

- **Concerns about Currency Manipulation and Trade Policies**

International relations may give rise to trade policies and worries about currency manipulation. Trade disputes and diplomatic tensions between nations may arise from accusations of purposely devaluing currencies in order to obtain trade advantages.

- **Effects on Interest Rates and Inflation**

Interest rates and inflation are influenced by changes in exchange rates. Central banks may decide to change interest rates in response to increased inflation brought on by a declining currency. The cost of borrowing and economic activity are affected by these changes.

- **Exchange rates and the state of the global economy**

Exchange rates can be impacted by broader changes in the world economy, such as recessions or recoveries. Currency values can be impacted by shifts in interest rates, geopolitical events, and global demand, which can then have an impact on trade balances across borders.

2. Finance Flows and Investor Confidence

The topic of capital flows and investor confidence is also covered. The way that investors perceive a nation's economic stability is significantly influenced by its currency fluctuations. This section examines the ways in which fluctuations in currency values can either encourage or discourage foreign investment.

- **Speculative Investor Attraction**

An investor seeking to profit from changes in exchange rates may be drawn to currency volatility. Speculative investments can be volatile, so while they may result in short-term cash inflows, they may not always support long-term development initiatives or economic growth.

- **High Risk for Investors from Other Countries**

For overseas investors, currency fluctuations bring extra risk. Because it is difficult for investors to predict returns with precision due to fluctuations in exchange rates, they may be discouraged from investing in projects in the affected country.

- **Impact on FDI, or Foreign Direct Investment**

Currency stability has an impact on foreign direct investment (FDI) often. Capital commitment to long-term development projects is more likely in nations with relatively stable currencies, as this lowers the risk of currency-related losses.

• Fears About Capital Flights

Constant currency volatility can cause capital flight, a phenomenon in which investors flee a nation because of increased unpredictability. This may have a detrimental effect on funding availability for development initiatives and impede economic expansion.

• Effect on Loan Interest Rates

Currency volatility affects borrowing prices for countries that depend on outside funding. A nation may pay higher interest rates when borrowing money abroad if its currency depreciates dramatically, which would raise the cost of funding development projects.

• Multinational Companies (MNCs') Confidence

When determining whether to invest in a foreign market, multinational corporations consider the stability of the currency. MNCs' confidence may be damaged by currency volatility, which could influence their choice to launch operations or take on significant projects in the impacted nation.

- **Reducing Foreign Exchange Risk**

To reduce the risk of currency fluctuations, multinational corporations frequently employ a range of financial instruments. Currency volatility can affect the availability and efficacy of these instruments, which in turn affects investors' willingness to commit capital.

- **Trade Balance and Economic Stability Affected**

Economic stability can be impacted by currency volatility, which can also affect a country's trade balance. A worsening trade balance might make a nation more dependent on foreign investment and more susceptible to the damaging effects of capital flight during uncertain times.

- **Governmental Reaction Policy**

An important factor is the government's response to currency volatility. Putting in place sensible fiscal and monetary policies are examples of effective policy measures that can reduce volatility, boost investor confidence, and draw in more steady foreign investment.

- **Economic and Political Stability are perceived to be stable**

Currency volatility can have an impact on a country's perception of its economic and political stability. Investors may be more willing to commit capital to countries with stable currencies, viewing them as safer places to make long-term investments.

- **Investment Decisions for the Long Term**

Currency stability is an important factor for long-term investors. Nations with stable currencies are more likely to attract investors interested in long-term projects that contribute to long-term economic development.

- **International Financial Institution Collaboration**

Countries experiencing currency volatility may seek support and stability from international financial institutions. By collaborating with these institutions, you can gain access to capital, technical assistance, and policy guidance, all of which can help your business grow.

3. Travel and Earnings in Foreign Currency

This chapter explores the relationship between currency fluctuations and tourism and how it affects a nation's appeal as a travel destination. Although devaluing one's currency can increase a nation's appeal to foreign visitors, there are drawbacks, such as increased expenses for departing tourists. The story skilfully strikes a balance between promoting tourism and controlling the financial effects of exchange rate swings.

- **Revenue from Tourism and Currency Changes**

Tourists' purchasing power may be impacted by currency fluctuations. In contrast, an appreciating currency may discourage tourists owing to higher costs, while a declining currency may draw in more foreign visitors looking for inexpensive travel experiences.

- **The Tourism Sector's Competitiveness**

A nation's tourist industry is more competitive when its currency is stable.
Consistent growth in tourism revenue is facilitated by predictable exchange rates, which give confidence to both travelers and hospitality industry businesses.

- **Effect on Spending by Tourists**

Travelers' purchasing decisions are influenced by changes in currency. When residents find foreign destinations more affordable, a stronger local currency may encourage outbound travel, but a weaker currency may encourage inbound travel as foreign visitors perceive the destination to be more cost-effective.

- **The Economic Benefits of Tourism**

A country's economy is greatly influenced by tourism. Currency stability promotes economic growth by ensuring a consistent flow of tourism-related income, which in turn supports nearby companies and creates job opportunities.

- **Effects of Infrastructure Investment in Tourism**

Investment choices in tourism infrastructure can be impacted by changes in exchange rates. Long-term investments in lodging, transit, and tourist attractions are encouraged by a stable currency environment, promoting tourism-related growth that is sustainable.

- **Tariffing Techniques for Travel Agencies**

Adaptive pricing strategies are imperative for tourism businesses due to currency fluctuations. Businesses that exercise pricing flexibility are able to manage profit margins and remain competitive by modifying rates in response to fluctuations in exchange rates.

- **Effect on Medium-Sized and Small Businesses (SMEs)**

The tourism industry's small and medium-sized businesses might be particularly susceptible to exchange rate changes. Unexpected fluctuations in currency exchange rates may have an impact on their pricing policies, operating expenses, and general competitiveness.

- **Marketing and Promotion of Travel**

An environment that is favorable for efficient marketing and promotion of travel is created by stable currencies. Consistent exchange rates improve marketing campaigns' effectiveness by drawing in a steady flow of visitors without raising eyebrows about sudden fluctuations in costs.

- **Utilizing Tourism to Promote Economic Diversification**

Economic diversification can be achieved through the use of tourism. In order to attract a wide variety of foreign visitors and lessen reliance on particular industries, a stable currency helps with efforts to diversify the economy.

- **Controlling the Pressures of Inflation**

Tourism-related inflationary pressures are lessened with the support of stable currencies. Surprising devaluations of currencies can raise prices in the tourism industry, impacting the cost of goods and services for visitors from both abroad and domestically.

- **Partnership with the Hotel Sector**

In order to manage currency fluctuations, governments work with the hospitality industry.

Tourism can grow sustainably when there is a concerted effort to implement flexible pricing strategies, offer incentives, and tackle issues associated with exchange volatility.

- **Combining Global Economic Policy with Integration**

To properly manage currency implications, tourism policies must be integrated with more general economic policies. In this way, stability and resilience against exchange rate fluctuations are fostered and tourism development is guaranteed to be in line with broader economic objectives through concerted efforts.

4. International Relations and Debt Servicing

Finding out how changes in exchange rates affect a nation's capacity to pay off its foreign debts becomes a central focus of the impact of currency fluctuations on debt servicing. Highlighting the challenging negotiations and policy considerations involved, the chapter examines the diplomatic and economic ramifications of managing debt in the face of exchange rate volatility.

- **Trustworthiness and Diplomatic Relations**

Negotiating sensitively with creditors is necessary when managing debt in the face of currency volatility. In the international financial community, a country's credibility and diplomatic relations can be negatively impacted by how it manages its debt, which can have an effect on future borrowing opportunities.

- **Debt Restructuring Negotiations**

Negotiations for debt restructuring may be necessary due to currency volatility. Restructured debt terms, like longer repayment terms or lower interest rates, are frequently discussed with creditors by nations experiencing economic difficulties brought on by currency fluctuations.

- **Juggling Debt Service and Economic Stability**

The task of balancing debt service obligations with economic stability falls to policymakers. Currency fluctuations can affect a country's capacity to pay its debts, so careful planning of fiscal policies is necessary to preserve stability and fulfill financial obligations.

- **Effect on Ratings of Credit**

Credit ratings are influenced by how a nation handles its debt in the face of exchange rate fluctuations. Credit reductions can lead to increased borrowing costs and a decline in confidence from foreign investors, which makes debt management plans more difficult to implement.

- **Arrangements with Global Financial Institutions**

Coordinating with global financial organizations like the International Monetary Fund (IMF) is common practice for countries facing currency volatility. Collaborative endeavors could encompass the pursuit of financial aid packages, policy recommendations, and assistance in executing efficacious debt management tactics.

- **The Issue of Sovereign Bonds and the Trust of Investors**

Sovereign bond issuance is a debt management tool, but investor confidence is impacted by currency volatility. To preserve investor trust, policymakers must carefully craft bond offerings, taking currency risks into account, and communicate in a transparent manner.

- **Economic Policy Repercussions**

Aligning debt management with more comprehensive economic policies is necessary in the face of currency volatility. Politicians need to take into account how debt management techniques support initiatives aimed at addressing structural problems, encouraging growth, and stabilizing the economy.

- **Perspectives from Politics and the Public**

Decisions about debt management have political ramifications because they affect how the public views and supports government initiatives. Gaining public acceptance and understanding of the reasoning behind debt management techniques requires effective communication.

- **Trade-offs between Stimulus and Austerity**

Nations that experience fluctuations in their currencies frequently struggle with balancing measures between stimulus and austerity. It is important to carefully weigh the short- and long-term effects of any decision regarding whether to reduce government spending to pay down debt or to enact stimulus packages to promote economic growth.

- **Execution of Structural Adjustments**

In the face of currency volatility, countries may need to enact structural reforms to address their debt problems. To increase resilience against external shocks, these reforms could strengthen economic fundamentals, increase transparency, and improve fiscal discipline.

- **Global Collaboration and Debt Reduction**

Debt relief initiatives could arise from cooperative efforts with creditors and international partners. In order to lessen the burden of debt service in the face of economic difficulties, countries may negotiate debt restructuring agreements or look to their creditors for assistance.

- **Systems for Monitoring and Early Warning**

Effective debt management implementation necessitates reliable monitoring and early warning systems. To make well-informed decisions and take proactive measures to address potential challenges, policymakers require up-to-date information on economic indicators, currency movements, and debt levels.

5. Exchange Rate Policies and Central Bank Interventions

An analysis is conducted on how central banks contribute to or exacerbate currency fluctuations. This section looks at the different instruments that central banks use to control or stabilize the value of their currencies, such as exchange rate policies and interventions. The chapter provides insight into the challenges of striking a balance between the need to maintain a competitive international position and domestic economic goals.

- **Policies for Exchange Rates**

Careful consideration of exchange rate policies is necessary to strike a balance between national economic goals and global competitiveness. Export competitiveness, inflation, and general economic stability are all impacted by decisions about whether to keep an exchange rate that is fixed, floating, or managed.

- **Priorities for the Budget and Fiscal Policies**

Social welfare, income inequality, and unemployment are examples of domestic economic goals that are frequently addressed. Strategic fiscal policies that allocate resources efficiently while preserving a competitive business environment are necessary to strike a balance between these goals and international competitiveness.

- **Protectionism and Trade Policy**

To strike a balance between national interests and global competitiveness, policymakers must manage trade policies. Promoting homegrown industries without using protectionism, which can exacerbate trade disputes and have a detrimental effect on global competitiveness, is a difficult task.

- **Corporate Competitiveness and the Regulatory Environment**

The regulatory landscape has a big impact on how competitively strong businesses are. Maintaining consumer protection, environmental sustainability, and business-friendly environment all need to be balanced for the sake of national and global competitiveness.

- **Skills Development and Labor Market Policies**

It takes efficient labor market policies to address domestic employment issues while preserving global competitiveness. Putting money into education, workforce training, and skill development helps find a balance between creating a skilled labor force that will make the country competitive in the global market and addressing employment needs at home.

- **Investment in Research and Innovation**

It takes research and innovation spending to strike a balance between national economic goals and global competitiveness. Encouraging technological innovation boosts a country's competitiveness on the world stage and stimulates domestic economic growth.

- **Monetary Policy and Targets for Inflation**

The task of developing monetary policies that strike a balance between national economic stability and global competitiveness falls on central banks. Currency values are impacted by interest rate management and inflation targets, which in turn affect a nation's ability to compete on the world market.

- **Development of Infrastructure and Connectivity**

The development of infrastructure is essential for both national economic expansion and global competitiveness. Investing in infrastructure that promotes both regional development and improved access to international markets is part of balancing priorities.

- **Sustainability of the Environment and Green Initiatives**

It's critical to strike a balance between environmental sustainability and economic growth. In a time when environmental concerns are becoming more and more important, policies that support green initiatives and sustainable practices boost both national well-being and competitiveness abroad.

- **Policy on Taxes and Business Taxation**

Policies related to climate change are crucial in striking a balance between national economic goals and global competitiveness. Encouraging investment and entrepreneurship while ensuring that tax laws comply with global norms is achieved by establishing a business-friendly tax environment.

- **Handling External Debt and Budgetary Control**

Sustaining fiscal restraint is crucial for striking a balance between national economic priorities and global competitiveness. Reliability in managing external debt guarantees a country's continued appeal to foreign creditors and investors.

- **Trends in the World Economy and Flexibility**

The capacity to adjust to worldwide economic patterns is essential for striking a balance between national goals and global competitiveness. To stay competitive in changing markets, policymakers must keep an eye on changes in the global economic scene and adapt their strategies accordingly.

6. International Economic Interdependence

The interdependence of the world economy and how changes in a nation's currency affect the larger international financial system are highlighted in this chapter. It explores how countries, international organizations, and financial institutions have worked together to address currency-related issues, demonstrating how crucial coordinated actions are to preserving the stability of the world economy.

• Reducing Systemic Hazards

Mitigating systemic risks that have the potential to impact the entire global economy requires coordinated responses. By working together, the possibility of significant economic consequences is decreased when tackling issues like financial crises, pandemics, and geopolitical unpredictability.

• Handling Cross-Border Issues

The stability of the world economy depends on concerted efforts to resolve cross-border issues. To reduce negative effects on economies throughout the world, cooperative solutions are needed for problems like cyber threats, climate change, and tensions in international trade.

• Sustaining Trust in the Financial Markets

Coordination of responses contributes to the preservation of financial market trust. In times of volatility, coordinated actions by international organizations, financial regulators, and central banks reassure investors and stabilize financial systems, preventing widespread panic and disruption of the market.

- **Planning for Emergencies and Crisis Management**

For crisis management and emergency preparation to be successful, coordinated responses are essential. In order to ensure a more robust and stable global economy, international organizations, governments, and central banks can collaborate to design and implement strategies to navigate economic downturns.

- **Encouragement of Open Markets and Trade**

Coordination of trade and open market promotion initiatives benefits global economic stability. Reduced barriers and increased international trade are two ways that multilateral agreements, free trade initiatives, and collaboration on trade policies support economic growth and stability.

• Aligning Monetary Measures

It is imperative that major economies coordinate their monetary policies. Currency wars and imbalances that could upset the balance of the world economy are less likely when interest rates and exchange rate policies are in line, thereby preventing competitive devaluations.

• Early Warning and Crisis Prevention Systems

The development of early warning systems and crisis prevention mechanisms is facilitated by coordinated responses. Nations are able to anticipate and mitigate new risks to economic stability before they become more serious thanks to timely information sharing and cooperative risk assessments.

• Assisting Emerging Markets

In order to support developing economies, coordinated efforts are essential. Collaboratively, developed nations and international organizations can offer financial support, technical assistance, and capacity-building initiatives to promote equitable global economic growth.

- **Improving Financial Supervision and Regulation**

Coordinated efforts to improve financial regulation and oversight assist global economic stability. Ensuring the resilience of the international financial system and preventing financial misconduct can be achieved through the implementation of uniform regulatory standards and supervisory practices across national borders.

- **Managing Health Crisis Worldwide**

Coordinated actions are necessary in the face of global health emergencies. In addition to improving public health, cooperative efforts in pandemic preparedness, healthcare, and vaccine distribution also promote economic stability by reducing interruptions to international trade and supply chains.

- **Cutting Down on Protectionism and Trade Barriers**

Reducing trade barriers and fighting protectionism are achieved through coordinated responses. In order to prevent the imposition of restrictive measures that could impede global trade and economic growth, multilateral negotiations and agreements are used to promote fair trade practices.

- **Enhancing Bilateral Organizations**

Responses that are coordinated improve multilateral institutions. Encouraging institutions like the World Bank, World Trade Organization, and International Monetary Fund (IMF) can better deliver financial support, stability, and global dispute resolution.

Fundamentally, investigating a nation's currency volatility on a global scale reveals a complex web of diplomatic, economic, and geopolitical factors. This chapter delves into the complex interrelationships among exchange rates, international trade, investor confidence, and the myriad factors that influence a nation's standing in the global economic arena.

Chapter 5

Managing Market Volatility

In a real estate market that is unstable, citizens must deal with a variety of issues, including housing security, moving, and wider social ramifications. These issues have a personal impact on people and families, but they also exacerbate broader social and economic divides in local communities. Comprehensive plans that take into account social justice, affordability, and the general well-being of the populace are needed to address these problems. Property values and affordability in the housing market are frequently impacted by economic instability. This chapter looks at the difficulties people have finding secure housing, moving, and dealing with the wider societal effects of a real estate market in flux.

1. Among the turbulence in the housing market is the affordability crisis

Because of the affordability crisis, citizens frequently encounter difficulties in obtaining secure housing. Housing prices can rise quickly as a result of real estate market volatility, making it more difficult for individuals and families to afford homes, particularly in urban areas.

2. Instability in the Rental Market

Instability in the rental market may be a result of real estate market volatility. Tenants may find it difficult to find stable and reasonably priced housing due to rent price fluctuations.

3. Displacement and Forced Relocation

Because of the unstable real estate market, citizens may be forcibly relocated or displaced. Communities can be disrupted and social dislocation can result from evictions brought on by redevelopment projects or rising property values.

4. Homelessness and Uncertainty in Housing

Homelessness and unstable housing can be exacerbated by real estate market volatility. Without stable housing options, people and families may have to rely on sporadic and unstable living arrangements or run the risk of becoming homeless.

5. Few Housing Choices for Communities at Risk

Vulnerable groups frequently take the brunt of a volatile real estate market, including marginalized communities and low-income individuals. Scarcely any affordable housing options lead to housing disparities and worsen social inequalities.

6. Stress and Burden of Finances

As housing costs rise, citizens may feel burdened and under financial strain. An excessive amount of income may need to be set aside for housing costs as a result of high real estate and rental rates, which leaves less money for other necessities.

7. Effects on Mental Health and Overall Welfare

The unpredictability and strain that come with a tumultuous real estate market can affect people's general well-being and mental health. Stress and anxiety are increased when there is housing instability, fear of being displaced, and financial strain.

8. Disturbances in Social Networks and Communities

Social networks and communities can be negatively impacted by real estate market volatility. Social tensions and a loss of community may result from forced relocations and changes in the neighborhood's demographics.

9. Difficulties in Becoming a Homeowner

Because of the volatility of the real estate market, citizens may find it difficult to access opportunities for homeownership. For those who want to own a home, high real estate costs and strict lending requirements may provide obstacles.

10. Effects on Children's Stability and Education

The education and general stability of children can be negatively impacted by housing instability. Relocating frequently can have an adverse effect on a child's long-term well-being by disrupting their social integration, academic performance, and attendance at school.

11. Pressures of Gentrification

In some neighborhoods, gentrification pressures may be exacerbated by real estate market volatility. Richer people and businesses moving in may force out existing communities and change the neighborhoods' cultural fabric.

12. Pressure on Social Services and Support Networks

Social services and support systems are put under pressure in a volatile real estate market. It may become more difficult to sufficiently meet the needs of the public due to an increase in demand for affordable housing initiatives, mental health services, and homeless shelters.

Uncertainty about Housing

In a volatile real estate market, this chapter explores the difficulties faced by citizens. People's struggles with affordability and shifting property values lead to a central theme of housing insecurity. In examining the difficulties faced by both renters and homeowners, this section highlights how real estate market uncertainty affects people's capacity to find stable housing.

1. Affluent Homeowner's Uncertainty

Homes can become unstable financially as a result of real estate market uncertainties. Property value fluctuations may have an impact on home equity, which can then have an effect on people's financial security and capacity to make wise homeownership decisions.

2. Affordability Issues with Mortgages

When the housing market is unstable, homeowners may have trouble affording their mortgages. Mortgage rates are subject to market and interest rate volatility, which could result in higher monthly payments and more financial hardship.

3. Sold Properties Difficulty

For homeowners, selling their properties can be difficult due to market uncertainties. When a person needs to sell their house, it might be more difficult due to lower demand, longer listing periods, and possible drops in property values.

4. Equity Issues That Are Negative

In uncertain times for the real estate market, homeowners may worry about negative equity. Homeowners' financial flexibility may be restricted if property values fall and they find themselves with mortgage debt exceeding the current market value of their properties.

5. Home Equity Is Hard to Access

Homes may have less access to home equity in uncertain real estate markets. People's ability to use their homes as collateral for loans or credit lines may be impacted by fluctuations in property values, which can also have an impact on the amount of equity available.

6. Renters' Experience of Rental Market Volatility

The volatility of the rental market impacts tenants who are subject to the uncertainties of the real estate market. A person who already struggles with affordability may find that their rent burden rises as a result of fluctuations in property values, which can affect rental prices.

7. Leash Renewal Insecurity

During unstable real estate market conditions, tenants may feel uneasy about their lease renewals. Renters may have concerns about future housing costs and stability as a result of landlords' ability to modify rental terms in response to changes in the market.

8. Restricted Rental Housing Options

Renters may have fewer housing options as a result of real estate market uncertainties. The number of reasonably priced rental units may be restricted by decreased building activity, tighter lending requirements, or changes in the ownership of rental properties.

9. Fear of Being Driven Out and Replaced

In times of uncertainty in the real estate market, both renters and homeowners may be afraid of being evicted and forced to move. A rise in worries regarding the stability of housing can be attributed to economic downturns or shifts in property ownership.

10. Impact on Housing Decision-Making

People's housing decision-making processes are influenced by real estate market uncertainties.

Due to worries about the volatile nature of the market, both homeowners and renters may put off making decisions about purchasing, selling, or relocating.

11.Stress on Personal Spending Plans

Both homeowners and renters may experience financial strain due to real estate market uncertainties. A person's ability to maintain overall financial stability may be impacted by having to devote a greater percentage of their income to housing expenses due to rising housing costs, whether they come from rent or mortgage payments.

12.Stress, Both Mental and Emotional

For both homeowners and renters, the real estate market's uncertainty adds to their mental and emotional strain. People's general quality of life can be negatively impacted by worries about housing stability, property values, and financial ramifications.

Pressures of Relocation

People are under pressure to move as the real estate market becomes more unstable. People considering or being compelled to relocate are influenced by a variety of factors, including job opportunities, economic conditions, and shifting property values. This section looks into the financial and emotional costs associated with moving, as well as the difficulties of adjusting to new communities and the possible disruption of social networks.

1. Anxiety and Emotional Stress

Anxiety and emotional stress can arise during the moving process. Sadness, anxiety, and homesickness are just a few of the feelings that can arise from leaving familiar surroundings, acclimating to a new environment, and facing unknowns in the future.

2. Financial Stress Associated with Moving Expenses

There are several costs associated with moving, including hiring movers, travel costs, and possibly temporary housing. Relocation expenses can be very expensive, which can have an effect on people's finances and budgets.

3. Effects on Mental Health

Moving has an emotional cost that can affect mental health. Feelings of loneliness or isolation, or even depressive symptoms, may be exacerbated by the process's stressors and the difficulties of adjusting to a new community.

4. Disturbances in Social Networks

Established social networks are frequently disturbed by moving. People might become socially isolated and find themselves in need of establishing new social networks in a new place if they are separated from friends, family, and other familiar support systems.

5. Difficulties with Adjusting to New Communities

There are difficulties in adjusting to new communities. People could find it challenging to navigate strange social dynamics, understand local customs, and make new friends, all of which can add to a feeling of alienation.

6. Adapting to Cultural Differences

Getting used to cultural differences could be part of moving to a new place. It takes time and work to understand local customs, norms, and community dynamics, and the process of adjusting may result in cultural shock and a feeling of being an outsider.

7. Familie's Transitions to Education

Moving may cause educational transitions for families with kids. For kids, adjusting to new schools, curricula, and peer groups can be emotionally taxing, which can affect their social and academic wellbeing.

8. Effects on Professional and Career Networks

Career and professional network changes are frequently associated with relocation. People might need to make new contacts in the workplace, which could have an impact on their career path and raise questions about their prospects for the future.

9. Loss of Routine and Familiarity

Changing places throws off daily routines. One may feel disoriented and find it necessary to establish new routines when they lose familiar surroundings, routines, and the comfort of knowing their community.

10. Prolonged Modifications and a Feeling of Authenticity

People's sense of belonging may be affected by long-term adaptations to a new setting. It could take some time for people to feel integrated and part of the community, which could have an impact on how happy they are with their new living arrangements overall.

11.Effects on Family Relationships

Moving can have an emotional and financial toll that affects family dynamics. Moving-related stressors can cause conflict within the family, so it's important to have open lines of communication and support one another as you work through the difficulties.

12.Managing Uncertainty and Change

People might find it difficult to adjust to the big changes and unknowns that come with moving. Creating healthy coping strategies, getting help, and keeping an optimistic view can all be very important in minimizing the financial and emotional costs associated with moving.

Access to Housing and Economic Disparities

The chapter focuses on how unstable real estate markets exacerbate economic disparities and expands its analysis to consider the wider societal effects. The growing divide between the wealthy and marginalized groups is partly caused by housing affordability issues, which disproportionately impact those with lower incomes. This section investigates the social consequences of uneven access to secure housing.

1. Rising Social Inequalities

Increased social inequality is a result of unequal access to secure housing. People with restricted access have difficulties meeting basic needs, which exacerbates socioeconomic group differences and divides communities.

2. Effects on Learning Possibilities

Opportunities for education may be impacted by unequal housing access. People who are homeless may encounter disruptions in their education, which could impact their academic performance and restrict their access to high-quality education, thus prolonging an unequal cycle.

3. Stress on the Nervous System and the Body

Both physical and mental health are strained when there is limited access to secure housing. People who are homeless frequently have higher stress levels, which can result in mental health problems. Inadequate living circumstances can also be a factor in physical health issues.

4. Disturbance of Social Unity

Inequality in housing access erodes community social cohesiveness. Inequalities in the stability of housing can lead to polarization, which intensifies social tensions and weakens the sense of common identity and interests within the community.

5. Effect on Employment Possibilities

Access to housing can have an impact on job prospects. People who don't have a stable place to live could have trouble finding and keeping a job, which would exacerbate economic inequality and impede social mobility.

6. Exposure to Homelessness

The likelihood of homelessness rises when people have unequal access to secure housing. Low-income individuals may be more likely to become homeless, which would increase their social marginalization and exclusion.

7. Fight for Equality in Society

People with unstable housing frequently find it difficult to integrate into society. Being socially isolated due to the stigma attached to unstable housing can make it difficult to fully engage in community life and activities.

8. Effect on Stability of Families

Unfair access to housing can cause family instability. Unstable housing can lead to family dissolution, which can negatively impact children's wellbeing and continue generations-long cycles of poverty.

9. Differences in Access to Local Resources

Inequalities in neighborhood resources are a result of unequal housing access. More stable housing tends to improve a community's access to services, employment opportunities, healthcare, and education.

10. Restricted Social Services Access

Limited access to social services may also be experienced by those who do not have equitable access to stable housing. Their struggles are made worse by this lack of assistance, which makes it more difficult for them to escape cycles of instability and poverty.

11. Social Mobility Affected

Social mobility is affected by unequal access to housing. Families and individuals with few housing options might find it challenging to relocate to places with greater opportunities, which would keep the concentration of disadvantage in particular areas.

12. Pressure on the Welfare of the Community

The well-being of communities is strained by the uneven distribution of stable housing. Inequalities in housing availability fuel social discontent, harming the general well-being and vitality of local communities and hindering attempts to create strong, resilient societies.

Stress and Mortgage Requirements

A crucial element of this chapter pertains to the financial strain that people encounter when dealing with an unstable real estate market. Property values fluctuate, which affects homeowners' equity and financial stability and makes mortgage burdens more noticeable. This section explores the possible fallout from mortgage stress, such as the possibility of foreclosure and the ripple effect on people and communities.

1. Anxiety and Financial Stress

Stress and anxiety are increased when people and families are under a lot of financial strain due to mortgage stress. The stress of having to pay a mortgage can have a significant negative impact on mental health, particularly in uncertain economic times.

2. Home Loss and the Risk of Foreclosure

The risk of foreclosure, which means losing one's home, is increased by mortgage stress. In addition to having an effect on a person's ability to maintain a place to live, foreclosure also causes families to be uprooted, which exacerbates the larger problem of homelessness.

3. Effect on Ratings of Credit

Individuals' credit ratings may suffer if they have trouble making their mortgage payments. Poor credit scores can prevent people from taking advantage of future loan opportunities, making it more difficult for them to get loans for things like cars, schooling, or other necessities.

4. Stress in the Family Unit

Family ties can suffer from mortgage stress. A family's overall well-being can be impacted by tensions and conflicts that arise from financial difficulties, especially those that are housing-related.

5. Community Stability is disrupted

The stability of communities is disrupted by foreclosures brought on by mortgage stress. Concentrations of foreclosed homes can cause neighborhood blight, which lowers property values and lowers community standards of living.

6. Reduced Value of Real Estate

A decrease in property values may be caused by the domino effect of mortgage stress. Homes not directly facing mortgage stress may suffer financially from concentrations of foreclosures, which can have a negative effect on the local housing market.

7. Economic Stress in Local Enterprises

Economic strain may be experienced by communities where mortgage stress is high. Reduced consumer spending as a result of financial hardships can have a detrimental effect on nearby companies and add to the community's ongoing economic problems.

8. Growing Need for Social Services

Social services can be a source of support for people who are stressed about their mortgage. Resources in the community are further strained by the rise in demand for financial counseling, mental health services, and housing assistance.

9. Influence on the Wellbeing of Children

Children's wellbeing can be significantly impacted by mortgage stress. Children's academic performance, emotional well-being, and general development may be impacted by the instability brought on by the fear of losing their home and financial strain in households.

10. The Battle to Restore Financial Stability

Foreclosed individuals might find it difficult to regain stability in their finances. Losing a home can have long-term effects that make finding new housing difficult and hinder an individual's ability to get back on their feet financially.

11. Disinvestment in the Neighborhood

Disinvestment in the neighborhood can result from mortgage stress and foreclosures. Potential buyers and investors become discouraged when properties go into foreclosure, maintenance deteriorates, and the neighborhood's allure wanes.

12. Social Exclusion and Shame

People who are stressed about their mortgages might feel isolated and stigmatized by society. The stigma attached to financial hardships can make people feel alone in their communities, which makes it harder for them to ask for help and exacerbates the emotional strain of their circumstances.

Social Fabric and Community Stability

The stability of communities and the foundation of society are all affected by the societal ramifications. Increased transience can be brought on by a volatile real estate market, which can undermine social cohesiveness and community. This section examines how changes in property values affect community involvement, neighborhood dynamics, as well as inhabitants' general well-being.

1. Socio Economic Profile of the Neighborhood

Neighborhood socioeconomic makeup is impacted by changes in property values. While falling property values may cause an exodus of residents and change the community's demographic composition, rising values may draw in higher-class residents and so contribute to gentrification.

2. Affecting the affordability of homes

The affordability of housing can be greatly impacted by fluctuations in property values.

While falling values might offer possibilities for affordable housing but might also indicate local economic difficulties, rising values might make homeownership more difficult for first-time buyers.

3. Tensions of Gentrification

The pressures associated with gentrification may increase as property values rise. Long-term inhabitants may be displaced as a result of higher-income people moving into ncighborhoods with increasing property values, which will change the social and cultural makeup of the area.

4. Participation in Community and Social Capital

Changes in real estate prices can have an impact on social capital and community involvement. Values that are steady or rising might motivate locals to make contributions to the community, which would build a sense of belonging and pride. A reduction in community involvement and disinvestment may result from declining values.

5. Neighborhood Renewal or Disintegration

Changes in property values can lead to a neighborhood's resurgence or downfall. While declining values may result in neglected properties and a reduction in the neighborhood's overall appeal, increasing values may draw investment and lead to better amenities and infrastructure.

6. Effects on nearby companies

Changes in property values have an impact on nearby companies. Raising values might draw in new investors and enterprises, promoting economic expansion. Reduced consumer spending, company closures, and local economic difficulties can result from declining values.

7. Possibilities for Residents to Receive Education

Residents' access to education is impacted by changes in property values. Raising property values may be correlated with more local funding for education, improving the quality of available learning resources. In contrast, falling values might lead to less money and difficulties in the classroom.

8. A feeling of safety and comfort

Trends in property values have an impact on residents' feelings of safety and wellbeing. While falling values may add to worries about real estate investment, safety, and the general well-being of the community, stable or rising values may foster a sense of security.

9. Effect on Local Government Assets

Variations in property prices have an effect on local government resources. Value increases might increase property tax income, giving towns more money for public services. Reduced values could put a pressure on municipal budgets, making it harder to pay for necessary services.

10. Social Unity and Confidence

Variations in property prices can have an impact on a community's trust and social cohesiveness. Growth or stability could increase trust between citizens and institutions, while declines could cause social unrest and a breakdown in the cohesiveness of the community.

11. Public Services and Amenities Accessible

Trends in property values have an impact on public amenities and services. A rise in values might encourage investment in infrastructure, parks, and public areas, improving the quality of life for locals. Reduced investment and restricted access to necessary services could arise from declining values.

12. Sustainability and Long-Term Livability

Variations in property values have long-term effects on a neighborhood's sustainability and livability. While negative trends could threaten the general sustainability and livability of a community, positive trends could help create one that is resilient and appealing.

Policy of the Government and Urban Design

This section addresses issues resulting from a volatile real estate market by looking at possible solutions and the role of urban planning and government policies. The article examines strategies to support affordable, stable housing, and sustainable development, highlighting the significance of taking preventative action to lessen adverse effects on individuals and communities.

1. Initiatives to Reduce Housing Costs

The challenges of housing affordability can be addressed by governments through policy implementation. To guarantee a variety of housing options for inhabitants, this may entail funding affordable housing developments, offering subsidies, or putting in place rent control laws.

2. Rules Regarding Zoning and Land Use

An important factor in determining the real estate landscape is urban planning and zoning laws. Using these instruments, governments can promote mixed-use developments, establish areas for affordable housing. Governments can also direct the general development of communities to accommodate a variety of population needs.

3. Rent Stabilization and Tenant Protections

Rent stabilization policies and tenant protections, such as restrictions on rent increases and measures to stop unfair eviction practices, can protect tenants during times of real estate volatility.

4. Affordable Housing Development Incentives

Governments can offer financial incentives to developers to create affordable housing, such as tax credits, waived permit fees, or other financial incentives. Community Land Trusts: Communities can establish community land trusts to protect their tenants during times of real estate market volatility.

5. Land Trusts for Communities

By establishing community land trusts, communities can manage and own land as a group, reducing the influence of real estate speculation. In the long run, this model can guarantee residents' affordability by stabilizing housing costs.

6. Transit-Based Development

Urban planning tactics can concentrate on transit-oriented development, which involves building high-density, mixed-use communities around public transportation hubs. This not only helps with the housing shortage but also encourages accessible and sustainable urban living.

7. Zoning for Inclusion

Governments can impose inclusionary zoning laws, which mandate that a predetermined proportion of newly constructed properties have affordable housing units. This guarantees that the commitment to housing a range of income groups will not change even as neighborhoods change.

8. Policies for Property Taxes

It is possible to affect real estate behavior through property tax policies. The maintenance of affordable housing units may be encouraged by tax incentives, owner-occupied home exemptions, or progressive property tax structures.

9. Protecting Cultural and Historical Legacy

To stop communities from being uprooted by gentrification, urban planning can prioritize the preservation of historical and cultural assets. Community identity is upheld by policies that encourage the preservation of existing buildings and cultural venues.

10. Reusing Adaptively and Redeveloping Brownfields

For the purpose of maximizing land use and reviving neighborhoods without adding to excessive urban sprawl, governments can support the adaptive reuse of existing structures and develop brownfields. Ecological and economical urban planning is in line with this strategy.

11. Boosting Renters' Rights

Renters will be treated fairly and protected from changes in the real estate market if their rights are strengthened by law. This covers rules pertaining to leases, upkeep requirements, and the eviction process.

12. Working Together to Plan with Stakeholders

Advocacy groups, developers, and members of the community are just a few of the stakeholders that governments can encourage to participate in collaborative planning. The needs and goals of the diverse population are taken into account in the development of housing and urban planning policies through inclusive decision-making processes.

In conclusion, this chapter deconstructs the complex issues that residents deal with concerning housing security, pressures to relocate, and the wider social ramifications of a real estate market that is unstable. It highlights the interdependence of these issues and the necessity of all-encompassing plans that take into account community well-being as a whole as well as personal struggles in the face of real estate market volatility.

Chapter 6

Financial Stress and Debt Burden

This chapter describes how citizens deal with financial stress, bankruptcy, and the long-term effects of debt accumulation in an unstable economic climate by examining the complex web of personal and national debt during unstable times.

1. Stress Related to Money and Coping Strategies

This chapter explores the profound effects of financial strain on people coping with an uncertain economy. It examines the psychological and emotional costs of economic instability and throws light on the different coping strategies people use to deal with stress. From financial restraints to concerns about employment. The diverse ways that people deal with the psychological toll that comes with unstable finances are captured in this section.

a. Planning Your Budget and Your Finances

People create and follow budgets as a coping mechanism for their inconsistent finances. A greater sense of control and a reduction in anxiety about unforeseen financial circumstances can come from better planning and money management.

b. Seeking Expert Guidance in Finances

A proactive approach to managing financial stress is to consult financial experts for advice. In order to help people through difficult financial times, financial advisors can offer advice on debt management, budgeting, and long-term financial planning.

c. Allocating Funds For Emergencies

One way to offer a financial safety net in uncertain times is to establish and preserve emergency funds. Reduced stress and a sense of security are brought on by knowing there are funds set aside for unforeseen costs.

d. Open Communication and Social Support

Emotional relief can be obtained by discussing financial worries with dependable family members, friends, or support groups. In addition to fostering understanding, open communication can result in cooperative solutions or support during trying times.

e. Looking for Assistance with Mental Health

Financial instability can cause a great deal of mental strain, so getting expert mental health support is essential. To manage the psychological effects of financial stress, therapists or counselors can offer coping mechanisms, emotional support, and a secure environment.

f. Building Coping and Resilience Capabilities

Developing coping mechanisms and resilience aids people in overcoming obstacles. This includes cultivating an optimistic outlook, adjusting to change, and discovering healthy coping mechanisms for stress, like mindfulness, meditation, or physical activity.

g. Examining Different Revenue Sources

Some people look into other sources of income as a way to deal with financial instability. To relieve financial pressure, this can entail looking for part-time employment, doing freelance work, or coming up with inventive ways to make extra money.

h. Setting Your Own Health First

Making self-care a priority is crucial for handling mental stress. People who lead healthy lifestyles with regular exercise, enough sleep, and stable finances are better able to handle the emotional toll that unstable finances take on.

i. Establishing Reasonable Expectations and Goals

It's critical to set reasonable financial expectations and goals. Realistic financial expectations can be less mentally taxing when one works toward attainable goals while acknowledging and accepting one's limitations.

j. Learning and Development of Skills

Putting money into education and skill development can boost people's self-esteem and employability. Expanding one's education or learning new skills can lead to more stable employment and career prospects.

k. Building a Network of Support

Creating a community or online support system can help foster a feeling of unity. Fostering a supportive environment for managing financial strain can be achieved through sharing experiences, advice, and resources with others facing similar challenges.

l. Putting Controllable Factors First

People who focus on things they can control are better able to cope with the psychological effects of unstable finances. A sense of empowerment can be generated by concentrating on doable tasks and tiny victories rather than wallowing in external uncertainties.

2. Economic downturns and bankruptcy

People frequently face the threat of bankruptcy as long as there is economic instability. The causes of these financial cliffs for people and companies are examined in this section. It examines the personal and legal ramifications of bankruptcy, highlighting how it can be used as a tactic to deal with overwhelming debt in difficult economic times as well as a result.

Some of the factors that push people and companies to these financial precipices are:

- **Financial Recessions**

Wider economic downturns can put people and businesses in danger of financial collapse. Economic downturns or recessions can lead to lower consumer spending, a decline in company activity, and financial difficulties for both people and companies.

- **Job Loss and Joblessness**

One major factor pushing people towards financial precipices is job loss or extended unemployment. Losing a reliable source of income can cause financial strain very quickly, making it harder for people to maintain their lifestyles and pay their debts.

- **High Debt Amounts**

Whether from credit cards, loans, or mortgages, racking up large debt amounts can put people and companies in risk of financial instability. Financial instability may arise from high-interest debt, particularly if timely payments are difficult to make.

- **Insufficient Emergency Savings**

People who don't have enough emergency savings are susceptible to financial crises. Financial distress can rapidly arise from unforeseen expenses like car repairs or medical emergencies if there is no safety net in place.

- **Inadequate Financial Management and Planning**

Financial precipices are a result of poor resource management and inadequate financial planning. Financial vulnerabilities can be made worse by inadequate financial planning, ineffective budgeting, or bad investment choices.

- **Mismanagement in the Business World**

Mismanagement, poor financial planning, inefficient cost control, or insufficient market research can cause businesses to experience financial crises. For businesses, these elements may result in decreased profitability and unstable finances.

- **Volatility of Markets**

Companies in sectors where market volatility is common may experience financial difficulties. Financial instability can result from variations in revenue streams and profit margins caused by changes in interest rates, commodity prices, or currency exchange rates.

- **Disruption of Technology**

Businesses that are unable to adjust to technological disruptions may face financial difficulties. Rapid technological advancements in certain industries could render traditional business models obsolete, putting companies in financial jeopardy and hindering their ability to innovate.

- **Health Issues**

Health crises can push people and companies to financial brink, whether they are personal or related to pandemics. Serious financial repercussions may result from medical expenses, lost productivity, and interruptions to business operations.

- **Regulatory and Legal Concerns**

Businesses may experience financial strain as a result of legal and regulatory issues. A person's or an organization's financial health may be impacted by fines, legal disputes, or regulatory changes that result in unforeseen expenses.

- **Insufficient Variety in Revenue Streams**

Financial risks can be incurred by people and businesses who depend too heavily on one source of income. A more solid financial foundation is provided by diversifying sources of income, which also lessens the impact of unforesccn difficulties.

- **Worldwide Crises and Events**

Global occurrences can have far-reaching effects on the economy, such as pandemics, natural disasters, and geopolitical crises. The wider effects of such events on the economy can leave people and businesses at financial precipices.

During hard times economically, bankruptcy can have the following effects on one's life and legal standing:

Bankruptcy's Legal Repercussions

- **Influence of Credit Score**

A person's credit score is greatly affected by filing for bankruptcy. For a number of years, a bankruptcy record may remain on credit reports, making it more difficult to obtain credit or loans in the future.

- **Disposition of Assets**

People filing for bankruptcy might have to sell off assets to pay back creditors. To pay off outstanding debts, this may entail selling real estate, cars, or other expensive goods.

- **Autonomous Staying**

A stay that stops creditors from pursuing collection actions is automatically triggered by filing for bankruptcy. This gives people time to straighten out their financial affairs and some short-term respite.

- **Paying Off Debt**

The possibility of certain debts being discharged is one of the main legal ramifications of bankruptcy. This provides a new beginning financially because the person is no longer obligated to pay back these debts.

- **Differentiating Between Options A and B**

Legal ramifications vary depending on the type of bankruptcy, such as option A versus option B. While option B consists of a debt repayment plan, option A comprises liquidation. The person's objectives and financial status will determine which option they choose between them.

- **Public Document**

The filing details for bankruptcy are made available to the public, and this could affect a person's standing both personally and professionally.

- **Bankruptcy Court Cases in Progress**

In court, the person filing for bankruptcy presents their financial status to the bankruptcy judge. It is frequently necessary to have legal representation during these proceedings.

The Personal Effects of Bankruptcy

- **Stress and Its Effect on Emotions**

Filing for bankruptcy can be a stressful and anxiety-inducing process. Shame and guilt about one's financial situation can be exacerbated by the stigma attached to them.

- **Boosting Credit**

People who file for bankruptcy have a difficult time getting their credit back. It could be challenging at first to get new credit, and people might need to develop responsible spending practices in order to become more creditworthy.

- **Restricted Possession of Future Credit**

Short-term credit access is restricted by bankruptcy. Even though some lenders might offer higher interest rates on credit, it could take some time for people to win back the trust of their creditors.

- **Housing and Workplace Difficulties**

Bankruptcy can have an effect on housing and job prospects. Credit history may be taken into account by some employers and landlords, which could make it difficult to obtain rental property or certain jobs.

- **Management and Education of Finances**

People who file for bankruptcy frequently evaluate their spending patterns and receive financial education. Gaining knowledge of sound money management becomes essential to averting such circumstances in the future.

- **Legal Charges and Fees**

There are associated costs and legal fees when filing for bankruptcy. People must take these costs into account when evaluating the total financial effects of filing for bankruptcy.

- **Effect on Co-Signers**

The bankruptcy filing may also affect cosigners on loans that the individual has signed. Co-signers might have to pay back the debt, and it might have an impact on their credit.

- **Future Difficulties with Borrowing**

People may have trouble getting good lending terms even after their bankruptcy is discharged. Because of the perceived risk involved with a bankruptcy history, lenders may offer credit with higher interest rates.

3. Debt Buildup and Its Long-Term Effects

The prevalent issue of debt accumulation and its long-term consequences are discussed in this chapter. For citizens who are forced to pay for necessities or unexpected emergencies, debt may be a coping mechanism. This section examines the compounding of debt, including the accumulation of interest, the impact on credit, and the long-term effects on people's financial prospects.

● Interest Amassed

Interest is charged on accrued debt, which increases the total amount owed over time. Excessive interest rates on credit cards and loans force borrowers to pay back more than they originally borrowed, which has a substantial effect on their dcbt load.

● The Snowball Effect

The snowball effect of compounding debt is a phenomenon in which interest on pre-existing debt adds to an already mounting debt load. People may find it difficult to make significant progress toward repaying the principal amount as a result.

● Impact of Credit Score

Credit scores can be negatively impacted by having large debt loads. Credit scores are impacted negatively by late payments, defaults, and high credit utilization ratios, which makes it more difficult for borrowers to get future credit or loans on favorable terms.

- **Restricted Credit Access**

Credit availability may be restricted for those with low credit scores. When lenders do offer credit cards or loans, it's usually at higher interest rates, which makes the debt load even heavier.

- **Having Trouble Getting a Loan**

One long-term effect of debt is that it makes it harder to get loans for important life events like buying a house or paying for schooling. People who have a history of excessive debt may find it difficult to get approved for these loans or to get favorable terms.

- **Impact of Stress on Mental Health**

Debt's compounding effects can exacerbate stress and have a detrimental effect on mental health. Anxiety can be caused by ongoing financial strain, the worry of getting into more debt, and the incapacity to fulfill financial commitments.

- **Tense Interactions**

Relationship strain can result from financial strain brought on by mounting debt. Tension and disputes within families and among friends can result from disagreements over money, duty sharing, and the stress of debt.

- **Possibilities for Getting Rich**

Long-term debt can limit a person's ability to accumulate wealth. People may find that their income is diverted to debt repayment rather than savings or investments, which will hinder their ability to create long-term financial security.

- **Effect on Savings for Retirement**

Compounding debt can make it difficult for some people to make sufficient contributions to retirement funds. Repaying debt before investing for retirement can have a long-term impact on a person's financial security in later life.

- **Diminished Flexibility in Money**

Debt compounding limits one's ability to make purchases. People might not have enough money for unforeseen costs or opportunities. Being rigid with how you handle your finances can make you more vulnerable to crises or downturns in the economy.

- **Long-Term Budgetary Objectives**

Long-term financial objectives are not immune to the long-term effects of debt. The ongoing burden of debt repayment may cause a significant delay in or compromise on starting a business, buying a home, or financing higher education.

- **Intricacy Taking the Cycle Apart**

It can be difficult to escape the debt spiral of compound interest. It may be challenging for people to set aside money for debt repayment, which feeds the cycle and makes it more difficult to achieve financial independence and stability.

4. The Risks of Foreclosure and Housing Insecurity

The risk of housing insecurity and foreclosure is a significant factor for citizens struggling with financial stress in an unstable economic environment. The vulnerability of homeowners is exacerbated by fluctuations in property values combined with mortgage obligations. This section looks at how people deal with the possibility of losing their homes, how that affects families afterwards, and how increased housing instability affects society as a whole.

- **Anxiety and Emotional Anguish**

For both individuals and families, the possibility of losing their house can result in severe emotional distress and anxiety. Fear, tension, and a sense of insecurity about the future can arise when there is uncertainty regarding the stability of housing.

- **Disruptions within the Family**

Family life is disturbed by the possibility of losing a home. Relationships may become strained in families who are facing eviction, because routines, everyday life, and family members' general well-being are all impacted by the stress of unstable housing.

- **Influence on the Wellbeing of Children**

Children's wellbeing is negatively impacted by unstable housing. It can impede their general development, interfere with their schooling, and cause them emotional distress. Children may suffer long-term effects from frequent moves and changes in living arrangements.

- **Challenges of Displacement and Relocation**

Finding new housing can be difficult for people and families who are compelled to leave their homes. Moving can be challenging due to a lack of resources, competition in the rental market, and possible discrimination. These factors further exacerbate housing instability.

- **Stress in Money**

Financial strain is a common part of the home loss process. Financial difficulties for those facing eviction or foreclosure may worsen as a result of extra expenses, court costs, and credit damage. Making it more difficult for people and families to make ends meet.

- **Chance of Homelessness**

The likelihood of homelessness rises with housing instability. If they can't find another place to live, people and families might end up homeless and have to deal with the difficulties of living on the streets.

- **Disturbances in Education**

Uncertainty in housing can cause educational disruptions for families with school-age children. Kids who move around a lot might have to transfer schools, which could affect their social and academic development.

- **Pressure on the Mind**

Mental health issues may arise as a result of the possibility of homelessness and the ensuing housing instability. As people and families deal with the uncertainty of their living situation, anxiety, depression, and other mental health issues may surface.

- **Effects on the Stability of Communities**

Instability in the community is exacerbated by unstable housing. A community's general social fabric may be impacted by concentrations of foreclosures and evictions, which may result in disinvestment, elevated crime rates, and strained relations between neighbors.

- **Social Inequities' Reinforcement**

Social injustices are strengthened by housing instability. This perpetuates cycles of poverty and inequality by disproportionately affecting vulnerable populations, such as low-income people and marginalized communities.

- **A burden on the social services**

Social services are further burdened in communities where housing instability is on the rise. Increased demand puts a strain on the ability of food banks, shelters for the homeless, and other support services to help people in need.

- **Possibility of Social Unrest**

Social unrest may be exacerbated by ongoing housing instability. People who are facing housing crises can use activism, protests, or other social mobilization strategies to voice their dissatisfaction and call for changes in policy and housing justice

5. Safety Nets and Support from the Government

This section examines how safety nets and support programs provided by the government can lessen the difficulties that people encounter when there is a financial crisis. It looks into how well social programs, unemployment insurance, and financial aid work as a safety net against the worst effects of unstable economic conditions. It also takes into consideration policy initiatives meant to avert generalized financial hardship.

- **Benefits for Unemployment**

People who lose their jobs during financial crises can receive unemployment benefits from government support programs.These benefits help people meet their basic needs while looking for new job opportunities by providing short-term financial support.

- **Social Assistance Initiatives**

Social assistance programs, like Supplemental Nutrition Assistance Program (SNAP) and Temporary Assistance for Needy Families (TANF), provide food assistance and financial support to low-income individuals and families. These initiatives serve as vital safety nets in times of financial instability.

- **Aid with Housing**

Programs for housing assistance are one way that the government supports people when they face financial difficulties and help them keep stable housing. This could include subsidized housing options for the needy, rental assistance, or programs that prevent evictions.

- **Healthcare Awards**

In order to guarantee that people have affordable access to medical services, prescription drugs, and preventive care, government support systems frequently include Medicaid programs or subsidies. Access to healthcare is crucial during financial crises.

- **Small Business Assistance**

During economic downturns, governments support small businesses with grants, loans, or financial assistance programs. This promotes employment stability, helps businesses weather financial crises, and supports general economic stability.

- **Debt Reduction Plans**

Programs for government-sponsored debt relief may be put in place to help people who are struggling financially. To ease financial strain, this may entail debt restructuring, forgiveness, or short-term relief measures.

- **Programs for Education and Training**

During financial crises, governments may provide education and training programs to address labor market issues. Through these programs, people can learn new skills that increase their competitiveness in the rapidly changing job market.

- **Services for Mental Health**

Governments fund mental health services because they understand how financial crises affect people's mental health. To assist people in managing their stress and anxiety, counseling and therapy services are frequently funded by the government or offered through public health initiatives.

- **Financial Counseling Services**

These services, which are funded by the government, help people manage their money in times of need. In order to support long-term stability, these services provide advice on financial planning, debt management, and budgeting.

- **Funds for Emergency Relief**

To help people and families in need of immediate financial support, governments may set up emergency relief funds. These monies can be quickly used to deal with unanticipated emergencies or natural disasters.

- **Workplace Development Programs**

Governments fund workforce development programs to increase employability during economic downturns. This could entail forming alliances with companies, academic institutions, and training providers in order to match skill sets with industry needs.

- **Measures to Protect Consumers**

During financial crises, governments enact consumer protection laws to protect people from predatory behavior. In order to prevent exploitation during vulnerable times, this includes regulations on lending, debt collection, and financial products.

6. Empowerment and Education in Finance

The chapter explores the significance of financial empowerment and education as a proactive measure. It looks at programs that give people the information and abilities they need to manage a changing economy, make wise financial decisions, and fortify themselves against the long-term effects of debt accumulation.

- **Conscientious Decision-Making**

People who are financially educated are better equipped to manage their money. Comprehending ideas such as debt management, investing, and budgeting empowers individuals to make confident financial decisions.

- **Increased Knowledge of Finance**

All around financial literacy is improved by financial education. People who are knowledgeable about financial terminology, systems, and practices are better able to handle their money wisely and steer clear of dangers.

- **Appropriate Credit Administration**

Prudent credit management is a lesson learned via financial education. People get knowledge about how credit functions, how it affects credit scores, and how to keep their credit in good standing. Making wise decisions about borrowing is aided by this knowledge.

- **Skills in Budgeting**

Budgeting abilities are emphasized in financial education, empowering people to manage their resources sensibly. Setting up a budget encourages responsible spending, saving, and planning for short- and long-term financial objectives.

- **Debt Avoidance and Reduction**

One of the most important components of financial education is knowing the effects of debt and how to reduce it. With this knowledge, people can take proactive measures to prevent debt accumulation and work toward paying off existing debt.

- **Creating and Investing Wealth**

Understanding the principles of investing and wealth-building tactics are made possible by financial education. People get knowledge about risk management, various investment options, and the significance of long-term financial planning.

- **Retirement Strategy**

People who are not financially educated can make better retirement plans. Making wise decisions for a safe retirement is aided by knowledge of investment vehicles, retirement savings, and the compounding effect.

- **Being Ready for Emergencies**

The significance of emergency savings is emphasized in financial education. People are made aware of the importance of saving money for unforeseen costs, which acts as a safety net in hard times.

- **Entrepreneurial Strengthening**

Financial literacy is essential for prospective business owners. It gives people the skills necessary to launch and run a business, such as risk management, budgeting, and financial forecasting.

- **Affluent Stewardship**

Resilience is promoted by financial literacy. Financially literate people are less likely to experience negative effects on their overall financial well-being when dealing with unforeseen costs, job changes, and economic uncertainty.

- **Self-assurance in Talking About Money**

Having a financial education gives one more confidence when talking about money. People are more likely to consult financial advisors or family members when making financial decisions, to have discussions about money, and to solicit advice.

- **Less Susceptibility to Financial Abuse**

One's susceptibility to fraud and financial abuse is decreased by financial education. Well-informed people are more likely to spot fraudulent schemes, safeguard their assets, and make wise financial decisions.

- **Marginalized Groups' Empowerment**

In order to empower marginalized groups, financial education is essential. Providing underprivileged communities with information and resources improves their capacity to obtain financial opportunities and break the cycle of poverty.

- **Gender Equality in the Economy**

The empowerment of women economically is facilitated by financial education. It improves women's capacity to engage in economic activities, make independent financial decisions, and safeguard their financial future by giving them money, knowledge and skills.

- **The stability of society and the economy**

Societal and economic stability are enhanced by a financially educated populace. The overall financial load on communities and governments is decreased when individuals possess strong money management skills, as they are less prone to encounter financial crises.

All told, this chapter provides a thorough overview of how people deal with debt accumulation, financial strain, bankruptcy, and the long-term effects of such circumstances in the difficult environment of an unstable economy. In order to empower people facing economic uncertainties, it emphasizes the necessity of a multifaceted strategy that includes legal considerations, proactive financial education, government interventions, and emotional support.

Chapter 7

Challenges of Entrepreneurship and Business

Small companies and entrepreneurs face particular difficulties in an unstable economy. This chapter investigates the ways in which individuals who conduct business deal with ambiguities, run the risk of insolvency, and affect the overall state of the economy.

Handling Commercial Uncertainties

In the midst of economic uncertainty, citizens who conduct business encounter complex challenges that are covered in this section. It investigates the methods used by business owners to handle the unstable environment, such as flexible decision-making and business model adaptation. The story highlights how resilient and flexible one must be to withstand setbacks and continue operating in a market that is changing quickly.

• Modular Business Structures

Adaptive business models must be implemented in order to prioritize resilience. Businesses that can quickly innovate, pivot, and modify their strategies are better able to manage uncertainty and continue operating in a rapidly shifting economic landscape.

• A methodical diversification

Sturdy companies strategically expand their product lines. To lessen sensitivity to particular economic shocks and adjust to shifting conditions, this involves diversifying product offerings, target markets, and supply chains.

• Processes for Making Agile Decisions

Making decisions with agility is necessary for adaptability. Businesses are more likely to succeed in a constantly shifting economic environment if they can act quickly and decisively, based on market trends and real-time data.

- **Investing in Electronics**

Technology advancement and resilience are frequently linked. Businesses that make technology, automation, and digitalization investments are better positioned to increase productivity, adjust to changes in the market, and maintain business operations in a changing economic climate.

- **Adaptable Work Environments**

Promoting adaptable work practices is a key component of resilience. Companies are better able to adjust to changing work environments when they can smoothly switch between remote and on-site work, support flexible schedules, and use technology for collaboration.

- **Chain of Supply Agility**

Supply chain agility is prioritized by resilient businesses. This entails spreading out your supplier base, making backup plans in case of emergencies, and leveraging technology to improve supply chain visibility and responsiveness.

- **Emotional Readiness**

To be adaptable, one must be financially prepared. Firms that possess comprehensive financial planning, effective risk management tactics, and emergency reserves are more equipped to withstand economic fluctuations and continue their activities in difficult circumstances.

- **Never-ending Education and Talent Acquisition**

Continuous learning and skill development are promoted by resilient organizations. By doing this, employers can increase the flexibility of their workforce by ensuring that workers are able to adjust to changing job roles and industry requirements.

- **Client-focused Methodology**

Customers are given priority in businesses that emphasize resilience. Businesses can modify goods, services, and communication tactics to satisfy shifting demands and expectations by having a thorough understanding of customer needs and preferences.

- **Togetherness and Alliances**

Cooperative businesses value strategic alliances and teamwork. By creating robust networks both inside and outside the industry, one can better navigate uncertainties by pooling resources, expertise, and support.

- **Planning for Scenarios**

Proactive scenario planning is a necessary component of adaptability. In an economic environment that is changing quickly, businesses that undertake comprehensive risk assessments, scenario planning, and stress testing can foresee possible obstacles and create plans to overcome them.

- **Worker Engagement and Well-Being**

Employee engagement and well-being are given top priority in resilient organizations. An engaged and driven workforce can adjust to change more easily, which helps the business remain resilient overall in unpredictable economic times.

- **ESG (environmental, social, and governance) factors**

Businesses that prioritize resilience incorporate environmental, social, and governance (ESG) factors into their corporate strategies. By addressing environmental and social risks, sustainability practices not only meet societal expectations but also build long-term resilience.

- **Consumer Input and Market Watching**

Flexible companies constantly ask for and monitor feedback from their customers and market trends. They can use this information to modify their products, promotions, and internal business processes in response to changing consumer demands and market conditions.

- **Risk Management and Regulatory Compliance**

Strong risk management and regulatory compliance are essential to resilience. Businesses are better equipped to navigate uncertainty and continue operations in a shifting economic landscape when they keep up with regulatory changes and effectively manage risks.

Entrepreneurial Resilience and Bankruptcy Risk

Businesses face the constant threat of bankruptcy as long as the economy is uncertain. In addition to examining the variables that raise the possibility of bankruptcy, this section looks into how business owners deal with financial hardship. It draws attention to how resilient and creative entrepreneurs are in reducing these risks, from financial restructuring to investigating potential new product or market opportunities.

- **Restructuring the Finances**

Financial restructuring is one way that entrepreneurs demonstrate their resilience. To maintain financial stability during hard times, this may entail renegotiating terms with creditors, looking into debt consolidation, or putting cost-cutting measures into place.

- **The process of varying sources of income**

In order to reduce risk, resilient business owners diversify their sources of income. To lessen reliance on a single source of income, this could entail extending the range of goods or services offered, breaking into untapped markets, or investigating new business ventures.

- **Modifications to Business Models**

By modifying business models in response to shifting conditions, entrepreneurs exhibit their inventiveness. This could be switching to online platforms instead of traditional ones, implementing subscription-based business plans, or adopting cutting-edge strategies to satisfy changing client demands.

- **Strategic Alliances and Cooperations**

In order to exchange networks, resources, and expertise, resilient businesspeople establish strategic alliances and partnerships. Through cooperative endeavors, they can jointly overcome obstacles and seize new opportunities.

- **Accepting the Digital Revolution**

Entrepreneurs use digital transformation to demonstrate their inventiveness. Using technology, automation, and online platforms can boost customer satisfaction, increase operational effectiveness, and create new growth opportunities.

- **Quickness in Making Decisions**

A resilient business person makes decisions with flexibility. Making prompt and well-informed decisions, grounded in market insights and evolving dynamics, enables them to promptly adjust to unforeseen obstacles and leverage emerging prospects.

- **Consumer-Focused Innovations**

To remain relevant, entrepreneurs give priority to innovations that focus on the needs of their customers. Comprehending the requirements and inclinations of customers enables businesses to customize their offerings, guaranteeing long-term patronage and adaptability to shifts in the market.

- **A Proactive Approach to Risk Management**

Proactively managing risks is a trait of resilient entrepreneurs. This entails spotting possible risks, putting risk-reduction measures into action, and setting up backup plans in case of unforeseen events.

- **Lean Operations and Measures of Efficiency**

By implementing efficiency and lean operations strategies, entrepreneurs exhibit resilience. Financial sustainability in hard times is facilitated by streamlining procedures, maximizing resource utilization, and cutting superfluous expenses.

- **Pay Attention to Employee Well-Being**

Employee wellbeing is a top priority for resilient business owners. Acknowledging the value of a driven and involved workforce, they put policies in place to assist staff members, cultivate a positive work environment, and improve the resilience of the entire team.

- **Relationship Management with Customers**

Proficient customer relationship management is emphasized by entrepreneurs. Developing and preserving close relationships with clients results in a base of devoted clients that can be relied upon in lean times.

- **Ongoing Education and Skill Advancement**

Entrepreneurs that are resilient make investments in ongoing education and skill enhancement. They can effectively manage risks by learning new skills, keeping up with market developments, and adapting to industry trends.

- **Techniques for Crisis Communication**

Resilience is demonstrated by entrepreneurs through skillful crisis communication. Open and honest communication fosters confidence and trust among stakeholders, such as clients, staff, and investors, which helps companies overcome obstacles.

- **Business Practices That Are Sustainable**

Business practices that are sustainable are adopted by resilient entrepreneurs. By lowering the risks connected to sustainability-related problems, environmental and social responsibility not only supports long-term resilience but also conforms to shifting consumer tastes.

- **Support and Participation in the Community**

Involved in and supportive of their communities, entrepreneurs demonstrate their resourcefulness. Strong community ties promote goodwill, improve brand reputation, and offer a support system in trying times.

Economic Landscape Contributions

In spite of uncertainty, this chapter looks at how businesses support resilience and economic growth in a larger economic context. In addition to promoting innovation and a vibrant business environment, it looks at the role that entrepreneurship plays in job creation. In order to promote economic recovery and sustainability, businesses are essential, as this section emphasizes.

- **Creating Jobs**

Businesses, by creating job opportunities, play a critical role in driving economic recovery. Increased employment benefits not only individuals and families, but also overall economic growth and stability.

- **Technological Advancement and Innovation**

Businesses drive economic recovery by innovating and advancing technology. Investing in research and development, implementing new technologies, and cultivating an innovative culture all contribute to increased productivity and competitiveness.

- **Investment as Economic Stimulus**

Businesses play an important role in economic recovery by making large investments. Capital spending, infrastructure development, and expansions all contribute to economic stimulus, creating a multiplier effect across multiple sectors.

- **Market Growth and Commerce**

Enterprises propel economic recuperation by broadening their market reach and participating in global commerce. Businesses that focus on exports increase their competitiveness, generate foreign exchange earnings, and create new growth opportunities.

- **Creating Revenue and Making Tax Payments**

Companies bring in money and pay taxes to the government. Tax revenues are essential for maintaining and growing the economy as a whole because they finance social programs, infrastructure improvements, and public services.

- **The Growth of Small Businesses and Entrepreneurship**

The expansion of entrepreneurship and small enterprises is essential to the recovery of the economy. Small businesses and startups add vibrancy to the business scene, encourage innovation, and help create jobs.

- **Development of Communities and Social Effects**

Businesses address societal needs and challenges by fostering community development and having a social impact. The general well-being of nearby communities is improved by philanthropy, community involvement, and corporate social responsibility programs.

- **Adaptivity and Resilience**

Enterprises exhibit robustness and flexibility, which are essential attributes for managing financial difficulties. Sustaining growth and recovery are facilitated by the capacity for innovation, model reversal, and market adaptation.

- **Training and the Development of Skills**

Companies fund training and skill-development initiatives to give employees the tools they need to succeed in rapidly changing fields. An educated labor force boosts output and strengthens the economy.

- **Social and Environmental Responsibility**

Businesses that embrace social and environmental responsibility help to ensure economic sustainability. Corporate responsibility initiatives, moral business conduct, and sustainable practices all support long-term environmental and economic well-being.

- **Infrastructure Construction**

Enterprises are essential to the development of infrastructure. Infrastructure expenditures, such as those for energy, transportation, and communication networks, not only generate employment but also set the stage for long-term economic expansion.

- **Capital Allocation and the Financial Markets**

Companies play a major role in the financial markets by helping with investment and capital allocation. Robust financial markets facilitate economic recuperation by directing capital towards profitable endeavors and stimulating entrepreneurial activity.

- **Consumer Spending and Confidence**

Businesses influence consumer confidence and spending, which aids in the economic recovery. Consumer trust is enhanced by a flourishing business environment, which raises spending and stimulates the economy.

- **Worldwide Competitivity**

Companies can become more globally competitive by implementing best practices, encouraging innovation, and entering foreign markets. On a larger scale, this worldwide involvement supports sustainability and economic resilience.

- **Extended Economic Forecasting**

Enterprises are involved in the long-range financial strategy. A vision for sustained economic growth is shaped by strategic business decisions, investments, and partnerships; these actions lay the foundation for a resilient and sustainable future.

Creativity and Adjustment

When faced with uncertainty, businesses frequently turn to creativity and adaptability. This section explores case studies and real-world instances of companies that have successfully changed course or implemented creative fixes to deal with difficult financial situations. It draws attention to how important inventiveness and progressive thinking are to prospering in a state of economic uncertainty.

Businesses that have effectively implemented creative solutions to overcome economic challenges include the following examples:

- **Pivot on Netflix**

With great success, Netflix changed its business model from renting DVDs by mail to becoming a massive streaming service. Acknowledging the shift in consumer preferences towards internet streaming, Netflix made significant investments in original content, building an extensive collection of films and television series. This calculated risk took the business by surprise and changed the entertainment sector.

- **Innovation on Amazon**

Originally an online bookshop, Amazon has since grown to become the biggest online marketplace in the world. Furthermore, advancements like Amazon Web Services (AWS) made the business a dominant force in cloud computing. Amazon's resilience in navigating economic challenges can be attributed to its ongoing innovation and diversification of offerings.

- **Pivot: Adobe**

Adobe Creative Cloud successfully transitioned from a traditional software sales model to a subscription-based model. This shift enabled the company to provide regular software updates and improvements, ensuring a consistent revenue stream. The subscription model increased customer engagement and market responsiveness.

- **Zoom: Creativity**

During the COVID-19 pandemic, Zoom became a household name. While video conferencing tools existed previously, Zoom pioneered a user-friendly platform to address the surge in remote work and virtual meetings. Its success demonstrates how businesses can innovate to meet new needs, even in difficult times.

- **Tesla is synonymous with innovation.**

Tesla shook up the automotive industry by introducing electric vehicles that were packed with cutting-edge technology. Tesla has expanded its business beyond automobiles to include solar energy and energy storage solutions. The company's innovation includes self-driving technology, demonstrating how innovation and sustainability can drive success in a competitive market.

- **Pivot from Airbnb**

During the pandemic, Airbnb successfully pivoted its business model. Airbnb shifted its focus to local and long-term rentals as travel restrictions impacted the hospitality industry. The platform was able to adapt to changing consumer preferences while also demonstrating agility and resilience in the face of economic challenges.

- **Pivot at Spotify**

By transitioning from a traditional ownership model to a subscription-based streaming service, Spotify transformed the music industry. This shift addressed not only changing consumer behavior but also piracy issues. Spotify's ability to adjust shows how important it is to recognize and react to market trends.

- **Innovation in Slack**

Teamwork was transformed when Slack unveiled a cutting-edge communication tool. Slack was a go-to tool for many businesses due to its user-friendly interface and integration capabilities, which were especially relevant during the rise of remote work. The success of the company underscores the significance of offering customized solutions for dynamic work settings.

- **Pivot by IBM**

With success, IBM changed its emphasis from hardware to software and services, where it now dominates the market. The company demonstrates its ability to adjust to the evolving technological landscape and maintain its competitiveness in the market by emphasizing cloud computing, artificial intelligence, and cybersecurity.

- **Nintendo: Creativity**

Nintendo has a long history of gaming industry innovation. The introduction of the Wii console with motion-sensing controls and the portable-console hybrid Nintendo Switch are two examples. Nintendo maintains its dominance in the gaming market by constantly reinventing its products.

The importance of innovation and foresight in not only surviving but thriving in uncertain economic times.

- **Product Innovation and Development**

Creativity drives innovation, which leads to the creation of new products and services. Businesses that think ahead focus on anticipating market needs, staying ahead of trends, and introducing novel solutions that set them apart in uncertain economic times.

• Models of Agile Business

Developing agile and flexible business models is made possible for businesses by creativity. In order to ensure resilience in the face of uncertainty, forward-thinking strategies entail developing structures that can quickly pivot in response to shifting market conditions.

• Market Diversification

One of the most progressive tactics is market diversification. Innovative methods for investigating new markets, populations, or clientele groups can give companies new sources of income and lessen their reliance on particular industries or geographical areas.

• Digital Conversion

In the digital transformation process, creativity is essential. Innovative companies use technology in novel ways to improve customer experiences, optimize workflows, and adopt digital platforms, setting themselves up for success in changing market conditions.

- **Consumer-focused innovations**

Customer-centric innovations are given priority by forward-thinking businesses. Understanding and satisfying customer needs creatively results in the creation of goods and services that appeal to shifting consumer tastes, encouraging client loyalty and business expansion.

- **Strategic Alliances and Cooperations**

Developing strategic alliances and collaborations requires creativity. Aspiring companies look for new and creative ways to work together, utilizing one another's assets and skills to help each other get through difficult times.

- **Data-Informed Judgmentation**

When making decisions based on data, creativity is utilized. Innovative companies use innovative data interpretation and analysis to learn about consumer behavior, market trends, and new opportunities, which helps them make strategic decisions.

- **Ongoing Education and Talent Acquisition**

Initiatives aimed at developing skills and promoting continuous learning make use of creativity. Creative skill development is an investment made by forward-thinking companies to make sure their workers are prepared to meet changing industry demands.

- **Taking Chances and Experimenting**

Innovative tactics encourage taking chances and trying new things. Businesses may quickly learn and adjust by using innovative methods to test new concepts, goods, or markets. This promotes an innovative and resilient culture within the company.

- **Planning Scenarios**

Scenario planning involves the use of creativity. Enterprises with a forward-thinking approach imaginatively investigate diverse situations and formulate tactical schemes to tackle possible obstacles, enabling them to effectively react to varying economic consequences.

- **Empowerment and Engagement of Employees**

Vibrant companies empower and engage their workforce in innovative ways. Businesses can access a variety of viewpoints that stimulate creativity and adaptability by cultivating a culture that values employee input and nurtures innovation.

- **Marketing and Brand Placement**

Brand positioning and marketing require creativity. Astute companies develop compelling brand identities that connect with customers, stand out from the competition, and creatively convey their value propositions.

- **Sustainability and Corporate Social Responsibility**

Ingenious companies combine sustainability and corporate social responsibility. Long-term corporate sustainability is aided by the application of creativity in the search for novel solutions that support social and environmental objectives.

- **Operating with Flexibility**

Businesses can develop adaptable operational strategies through the application of creativity. Innovative ways to optimize operations, cut expenses, and boost productivity are part of forward-thinking strategies, which guarantee flexibility in erratic financial environments.

- **Forecasting Upcoming Patterns**

Thinking ahead to future trends requires creativity. In order to stay ahead of the curve and be able to react quickly to shifting market conditions, progressive companies also employ innovative methods of analyzing social changes, new technologies, and market signals.

State Assistance and Its Effects on Policy

The narrative looks at the assistance and regulations provided by the government to companies in unpredictable times. The efficacy of financial assistance programs, regulatory actions, and stimulus packages in supporting entrepreneurial endeavors is examined. The effects of supportive policies on the entire economic ecosystem are also covered.

In times of uncertainty, the following are some ways that government policies and support can help businesses:

- **Programs for Financial Assistance**
During uncertain times, governments frequently offer financial assistance programs, such as loans, grants, or subsidies, to support businesses. These grants can assist companies with paying

for operations, keeping workers, and overcoming financial obstacles.

• Tax Breaks and Other Incentives

To lessen the financial burden on businesses, governments may enact tax breaks or other incentives. This can include credits designed to boost economic activity and give businesses more financial flexibility, tax deferrals, or lower tax rates.

• Pay Supplements and Job Initiatives

Programs for employment and wage subsidies are intended to incentivize companies to hire or keep workers during lean times.By supporting workforce stability and promoting overall economic resilience, these initiatives seek to reduce layoffs.

• Plans and Training for Business Continuity

Plans for business continuity and training initiatives are two ways that governments can assist. By offering tools and crisis management experience, these programs assist companies in anticipating and lessening the effects of uncertainty.

- **Adaptability of Rules**

In uncertain times, regulatory flexibility measures may be adopted by governments to reduce the burden of compliance on businesses. In order to help businesses adjust more readily to changing circumstances, this can include temporary waivers, extensions, or modifications to regulations.

- **Assistance Tailored to Industry**

Sectors that are severely impacted by uncertainty may receive targeted assistance from governments. Assistance may come in the form of specialized funding, regulatory relaxation, or joint projects to tackle issues unique to a given industry.

- **Infrastructure Financing**

In order to boost economic activity and open doors for businesses, governments may expedite infrastructure projects or fund public works initiatives. The economy as a whole can benefit from infrastructure spending in a number of ways.

- **Getting Finance and Credit Accessible**

Government support is essential in ensuring that businesses have access to finance and credit. Partnerships with financial institutions, guarantee programs, and low-interest loans can all assist businesses in obtaining the funding they require to weather difficult times.

- **Facilitating Trade and Export Promotion**

To support companies operating globally, governments can actively encourage exports and facilitate international trade. To open up new markets or remove trade barriers, this can involve trade agreements, export credit schemes, and diplomatic initiatives.

217

- **Resources for Research and Development**

To encourage innovation and assist companies in adjusting to shifting market demands, governments may set aside money for research and development projects. Resilience and competitiveness in the face of uncertainty are fostered by this support.

- **Safety nets for society**

Social safety nets that tangentially assist businesses are a function of governments. Demand for goods and services must be sustained, and programs like social assistance and unemployment benefits help to preserve consumer purchasing power.

- **Cross-Sector Collaborations**

Businesses can benefit more from public-private partnerships, which are collaboration between the public and private sectors. Partnerships can take the form of industry-specific projects that combine the advantages of both sectors, technology development, or infrastructure projects.

- **Interaction and Exchange of Information**

In times of uncertainty, governments can help businesses by communicating in a timely and clear manner. This involves educating people about economic policies, public health initiatives, and business resource availability so they can make well-informed decisions.

- **Limitations on Liability and Legal Protections**

In uncertain times, governments may impose liability limitations and legal protections to protect businesses from specific risks. By lowering the likelihood of legal issues and offering a certain degree of assurance, these actions can promote a more stable business environment.

- **Crisis Management and Arrangements**

When it comes to crisis response and coordination, governments are essential. In order to ensure a coordinated and effective response to challenges, task forces, emergency response teams, and communication channels should be established. This benefits both businesses and the larger community.

The following are the consequences of supportive policies on the overall economic ecosystem:

- **Investment and Business Development**

Policies that foster business growth and investment create a favorable environment. This encourages entrepreneurs and businesses to grow their businesses, invest in new ventures, and contribute to overall economic development.

- **Job Generation**

Business-friendly policies frequently result in job creation. A thriving business environment stimulates job creation, lowering unemployment rates and improving the population's overall economic well-being.

- **Research and Development**

Policy incentives encourage innovation and research development. When businesses have confidence in a regulatory framework that encourages and protects intellectual property, they are more likely to invest in research and development.

- **Enhanced Competitiveness**

Policies that help businesses increase their competitiveness. This is accomplished through measures such as tax breaks, simplified regulations, and increased access to resources, which allow businesses to compete more effectively in domestic and international markets.

- **FDI (Foreign Direct Investment)**

Foreign direct investment (FDI) is attracted by supportive policies. Governments that foster a business-friendly environment encourage foreign investors to bring capital, technology, and expertise into the country, thereby contributing to economic growth and stability.

- **Infrastructure Improvement**

Policies that help businesses are frequently aligned with infrastructure development. Governments can invest in critical infrastructure like transportation, communication, and energy, laying the groundwork for long-term economic growth.

- **Through Financial Diversification**

Economic diversification is facilitated by supportive policies. Policies help create a more resilient and diversified economy that is less susceptible to shocks in particular industries by promoting the expansion of diverse industries.

- **Growth of Small and Medium-Sized Enterprises (SMEs)**

Policies that assist SMEs encourage inclusive economic development. Small and medium-sized enterprises (SMEs), widely regarded as the foundation of economies, gain from policies that facilitate financing access, lessen regulatory burdens, and promote a favorable business environment.

• Ecological Methods

Sustainable business practices are encouraged by supportive policies. Long-term economic and environmental sustainability can be enhanced by governments enforcing rules and providing incentives to companies that adopt socially and environmentally responsible practices.

• Customer Confidence

Business-friendly policies help to foster consumer confidence. Consumer confidence is bolstered by a stable and prosperous business environment, which encourages higher spending and boosts economic activity.

• Area-Wide Progress

Disparities by region can be addressed by supportive policies. Governments may put policies into place to support economic activity in underdeveloped areas, encouraging more evenly distributed economic growth throughout the board.

- **Technology Acceptance**

Adoption of technology is frequently aided by business-friendly policies. Governments help to raise productivity and competitiveness in the global market by offering incentives for technological innovation and investments.

- **Stability of the Finance Markets**

Financial market stability is a result of supportive policies. In order to maintain the stability of financial markets, well-regulated financial systems and laws that support accountability and transparency also boost investor confidence.

- **Beginning-Up Culture and Entrepreneurship**

Entrepreneurship and a thriving start-up culture are fostered by supportive policies. Encouraging innovation, job creation, and dynamism injection into the economic ecosystem are all facilitated by creating an atmosphere that allows new businesses to flourish.

- **Economic Integration and World Trade**

Global trade and economic integration are improved by policies that are supportive. Policies that promote trade help a nation integrate into the global economy by providing new markets and business opportunities.

Industry Networks and Cooperation

Industry networks and teamwork are often powerful tools for entrepreneurs. This section examines the strategies that companies use to form alliances, pool resources, and work together to reduce risks. It looks into how industry networks and associations help, encourage innovation, and give businesses a bigger voice when it comes to promoting policies that benefit them.

- **Promoting Beneficial Laws**

Industry networks and associations are essential in promoting policies that benefit businesses. These groups can interact with legislators and shape laws that promote industry development and competitiveness by combining their combined clout and knowledge.

- **Best Practices and Information Exchange**

Businesses can more easily share best practices and information by joining industry associations. Businesses can share knowledge with one another in this cooperative setting, keep up with market developments and adopt creative strategies that can boost overall competitiveness.

- **Collaboration and Networking**

Industry associations offer venues for cooperation and networking. Companies in a given sector can network, work together on projects, and investigate possible alliances, creating a cooperative environment that encourages creativity and mutual success.

• Collaborative Issue-Solving

Industry associations facilitate cooperative problem-solving during difficult times. Companies can work together to solve problems together, pool resources, and create solutions that help the sector as a whole. This builds industry resilience when faced with shared difficulties.

• Obtaining Finance and Resources

Businesses can access vital resources and funding opportunities through industry associations. Joint research projects and industry-wide programs are examples of collective initiatives that can draw funding that helps several businesses, which promotes growth and innovation.

• Participation in Regulation-Related Conversations

In regulatory discussions, industry associations speak for businesses as a whole. By ensuring that the opinions and concerns of businesses are taken into account during the policy-making process, this representation fosters a more welcoming and cooperative regulatory environment.

- **Professional Development and Training**

Industry associations provide training and professional development opportunities. These groups assist companies in developing their workforce, keeping abreast of industry developments, and adjusting to shifting market conditions by planning workshops, seminars, and training sessions.

- **Gaining Entry into and Growing Within Markets**

Businesses can obtain assistance for entering new markets and growing their operations through industry networks. Associations can help companies navigate regulatory frameworks, lobby for advantageous trade agreements, and offer market intelligence, all of which can lead to opportunities for international growth.

- **Initiatives for Innovation and Research**

Research and innovation projects are frequently led by industry associations. Businesses can pool their resources to invest in innovation, technology adoption, and the creation of game-changing new solutions that benefit the entire sector by coordinating their research efforts.

- **Knowledge and Awareness of Policies**

Industry associations are essential in providing businesses with policy and regulation education. These groups equip companies to handle complicated regulatory environments and adhere to industry standards by dispensing resources and raising awareness.

- **Building Resilience and Managing Crises**

Industry associations help with crisis management and resilience-building in times of crisis. These organizations support businesses in navigating challenges and recovering more successfully by sharing best practices, coordinating responses, and offering support mechanisms.

- **International Forum Representation**

In international forums, businesses are represented by industry associations. Through collaboration with counterparts from various regions, global perspectives are fostered and businesses are able to stay informed about international trends, participate in global discussions, and work with counterparts from different regions.

- **Industry Promotion and Branding**

Associations for the industry take part in branding and industry promotion. These groups promote the industry as a whole to increase investment, increase public awareness, and improve the perception of companies operating in it.

- **Assurance of Quality and Standardization**

Associations for the industry help with quality control and standardization. By establishing industry standards, businesses can maintain the reputation of their sector and foster consumer trust by ensuring uniformity and quality across all products and services.

- **Knowledge Transfer and Mentoring**

Trade associations support the exchange of knowledge and mentoring. In order to promote a culture of learning, cooperation, and continuous improvement within the industry, established businesses can impart their knowledge and insights to more recent entrants.

All things considered, this chapter provides a thorough overview of how citizens who are involved in business activities deal with uncertainty, risk going bankrupt, and affect the overall state of the economy. The statement emphasizes the intricate relationship between personal entrepreneurship, financial stability, and the overall influence on the economic well-being of a country.

Chapter 8

Amplification of Social Inequality

This chapter explores how economic instability exacerbates social inequalities by examining the growing divide between the wealthy and the marginalized. Social divisions are exacerbated by the varied degrees of hardship faced by citizens from different socioeconomic backgrounds.

1. Wealth Inequalities

This section explores how social inequality is exacerbated by economic instability, which serves as a catalyst. It highlights how economic fluctuations disproportionately affect people and communities and examines the growing divide between the wealthy and the marginalized. When economic instability wears down, wealth disparities widen and feed an ongoing cycle of inequality.

• Inequality of Income

Changes in the economy frequently make income inequality worse by extending the divide between the wealthy and the marginalized. People with higher incomes might face less financial hardship during recessions, while people with lower incomes might encounter more serious difficulties.

• Gaps in Employment

When there is a recession, marginalized communities suffer disproportionately from job losses. An increasing number of marginalized and wealthy people have limited access to stable employment opportunities and are more vulnerable to layoffs.

• Obtaining Education

Access to education is impacted by changes in the economy, and marginalized people are more likely to face difficulties. Rich families might be able to afford to keep their children in school, but marginalized communities might face obstacles that prevent them from getting the education they need.

• Health Inequalities

Healthcare disparities are often made worse by fluctuations in the economy. Rich people might have easier access to high-quality healthcare resources and services, while underprivileged populations might face obstacles to care, which would worsen health outcomes.

• Uncertainty in Housing

Housing insecurity is exacerbated for marginalized communities by economic instability. Rich people might be better equipped to withstand changes in the housing market, but marginalized groups are more vulnerable to homelessness, eviction, and subpar housing.

• Assets and Wealth Accumulation

Differently, wealth accumulation is impacted by fluctuations in the economy. Rich people frequently have diversified portfolios that help them weather market turbulence, but marginalized people might not have the resources to accumulate and safeguard their wealth, which widens the wealth gap.

- **Debt and Stress Regarding Money**

During economic downturns, marginalized people are more vulnerable to debt accumulation and financial stress. These communities are more financially vulnerable due to a lack of financial safety nets, higher interest rates, and restricted credit availability.

- **Impact on Small Businesses**

Variations in the economy have an effect on small businesses, which are frequently essential to underprivileged communities. While small businesses in marginalized areas face closures, job losses, and diminished economic opportunities, wealthy entrepreneurs might have greater resources to weather economic challenges.

- **Resources for the Public and Social Services**

Social services and public resources are vital to marginalized communities. Inequalities in healthcare, education, and other critical support systems may worsen as a result of budget cuts and decreased funding for these services brought on by economic fluctuations.

- **Resource Access and Financial Literacy**

Rich people frequently have greater access to resources and financial literacy, which aids in navigating uncertain economic times. Communities that are marginalized might not have access to resources or information for education, making them more susceptible to the damaging effects of changes in the economy.

- **Impact on Generations**

Changes in the economy affect generations beyond one generation. While marginalized people may find it difficult to break the cycle of poverty due to a lack of resources and opportunities, wealthy families can offer stability and financial support to their offspring for generations to come.

• Utilizing Technology

Rich people might have easier access to technology, which would allow them to adjust to working from home and taking classes online when the economy is struggling. Digital divides may prevent marginalized communities from fully engaging in the changing economy.

• Psychological Health

Distinct effects of economic fluctuations on psychological well-being can be observed. Rich people might have more resources for mental health, but those on the margins might experience more stress, anxiety, and mental health issues because of unstable finances.

• Public Participation

Civic engagement can be impacted by economic disparities. Rich people might have more means to engage in politics, but marginalized groups might lose their right to vote and have less representation in the decision-making process.

• Community Hardiness

Communities are put to the test by economic fluctuations. Richer neighborhoods might have more robust social networks and resources to withstand economic downturns. On the other hand, communities that are marginalized are more vulnerable and at risk of social fragmentation.

• Disparities in employment

Economic instability frequently leads to unequal employment opportunities, which have varying effects on different skill levels and sectors. This section looks into how disparities in layoffs, wage stagnation, and job insecurity contribute to growing employment inequities. Social divisions may get worse for members of marginalized groups if they have more difficulty finding steady employment.

- **Uncertainty in the Job**

Marginalized people are disproportionately impacted by job insecurity, which exacerbates already existing employment disparities. These people frequently work in unstable environments, such as temporary or part-time jobs, which increases their susceptibility to layoffs and downturns in the economy.

- **Falling wages**

Employment disparities are worsened by wage stagnation. While marginalized people frequently see their wages stagnate, wealthy people may be able to negotiate higher salaries and have access to better-paying jobs. However, the wages of marginalized people are frequently stagnant, which restricts their ability to grow financially and keeps income disparities alive.

- **Variations in Terminations**

Differences in the number of layoffs increase during recessions. Deepening employment disparities, marginalized people may be more likely to experience job losses as a result of factors like industry concentration, discriminatory practices, and a lack of job security.

- **Obtaining Training and Developing Skills**

Unequal access to training and skill development can be a contributing factor to wage stagnation and disparities in layoffs. Rich people might have more resources available to them for lifelong learning and skill development, which would help them adjust to the demands of a changing labor market.

- **Discrimination in Promotion and Hiring**

Discrimination in hiring and promotion exacerbates existing employment disparities. Disparities in job security and pay may be sustained by marginalized people due to systemic obstacles that restrict their access to opportunities for career advancement.

- **Absence of Benefits at Work**

Workplace disparities are exacerbated by marginalized people's frequent lack of access to benefits. In order to improve their overall job security and well-being, wealthy workers may be able to negotiate better benefits, such as healthcare, retirement plans, and parental leave.

- **Obtaining Opportunities for Networking**

Access to networking opportunities affects disparities in employment. Rich people often have large professional networks, which gives them access to insider information about job openings and increases their chances of job security. This is not the case for people with smaller professional networks.

- **Racial Disparities and the Gender Pay Gap**

Employment disparities are exacerbated by the gender pay gap and racial wage gaps. Women and members of underrepresented racial and ethnic groups frequently face reduced pay, less opportunities for career advancement, and heightened susceptibility to layoffs.

• Curriculum Inequalities

Educational disparities are associated with wage stagnation and employment inequities. While marginalized people face obstacles to obtaining an education, wealthy people may have access to higher-quality education, which could lead to better job opportunities and higher earning potential.

• Lack of Flexibility in the Labor Market

An inflexible labor market exacerbates disparities in employment. Rich people might be able to handle unemployment for extended periods of time, but marginalized people have a harder time finding new jobs, which results in long-term job instability.

• Regional Inequalities

Employment disparities are exacerbated by geographic disparities. Rich people might have more opportunities in places with robust labor markets, while marginalized people in places with weak economies would have higher unemployment and less job security.

- **Discrimination in Employment Opportunities Access**

Employment disparities are sustained by discrimination in access to job opportunities. People on the margins may experience bias during the hiring process, which would reduce their chances of landing a steady job and drive down wages.

- **Restricted access to starting a business**

Limited access to entrepreneurship influences disparities in employment. Rich people might be able to launch their own companies and secure employment, but marginalized people have obstacles in their way when it comes to economic independence and entrepreneurship.

- **Absence of Diversity and Inclusion in the Workplace**

Employment disparities are a result of workplace diversity and inclusion gaps. Rich people might gain from diverse talent-recognized workplaces that are inclusive, but marginalized people might experience exclusionary practices that impede their career advancement and job security.

- **Economic Policy's Effect**

Economic policies have an impact on employment disparities. Policies that favor the wealthy over others or ignore structural injustices may exacerbate disparities in employment by causing wage stagnation and unequal layoff rates.

4. Education and Opportunity Access

One of the main concerns is how economic instability affects opportunities and education. This section examines how access to high-quality education, training programs, and skill development are impacted by economic fluctuations. People from marginalized backgrounds might run into obstacles that prevent them from taking advantage of opportunities, sustaining generational disparities in society.

- **Reduced Education Funding**

In the education sector, budget cuts are frequently the result of economic fluctuations. Lower public support for schools, colleges, and universities can result in fewer resources available for high-quality education, which can have an impact on the accessibility of educational opportunities and the general learning environment.

- **Higher Education's Affordability**

The cost-effectiveness of postsecondary education is impacted by economic fluctuations. People may have trouble paying for their education during economic downturns, which could result in fewer students enrolling in colleges and universities and restricting their access to advanced skill development programs.

- **Access to Training Programs Restricted**

Programs for training may become less accessible during economic downturns. Companies might reduce the amount of training they offer, restricting people's ability to learn new skills and making it more difficult for them to adjust to the changing needs of the labor market.

- **Effects on Career Education**

Programs for vocational education may be impacted by changes in the economy. Access to opportunities for vocational education may be restricted during economic downturns due to reduced funding for vocational training institutions and decreased demand for particular skills, especially for those seeking practical, job-oriented skills.

- **Budgets for corporate training are declining**

Budgets for training may be trimmed by corporations during uncertain economic times. This may limit workers' access to opportunities for professional growth and impede workplace skill-enhancement initiatives.

- **Financial Assistance and Limited Scholarships**

Financial assistance and scholarships may become less accessible during recessions. Access to higher education for some people, especially those from economically disadvantaged backgrounds, may be restricted due to reduced funding for grants and scholarships related to education.

- **Facilities for Education**

The creation and upkeep of educational infrastructure may be impacted by changes in the economy. The quality of education offered may suffer if schools and training facilities are slow to upgrade their infrastructure and integrate new technologies.

- **Reduced Placement Services for Jobs**

Recessions in the economy may cause educational institutions to offer fewer job placement services. With fewer resources, students may receive less assistance in locating jobs after completing their training or education programs.

- **Changes in the Need for Skills**

Changes in the economy can cause a shift in the need for particular skills. Businesses that are going through a downturn might need different skill sets, which would affect the value of the current educational and training programs and people's capacity to match their skills to what employers are looking for.

- **Research and Development Program Impact**

Programs for research and development in educational institutions may be impacted by changes in the economy. Cuts to research initiative funding may make it more difficult to develop cutting-edge skills and prevent the development of novel training approaches.

- **The Education Digital Gap**

A recession may exacerbate the educational digital divide. A lack of resources could make it more difficult for schools to implement technology, which would affect access to online learning environments and disadvantage students who don't have the required digital tools.

- **Decline in Opportunities for Professional Development**

Teachers may have fewer opportunities for professional development as a result of economic uncertainty. Insufficient funds for continuing professional development and teacher training can have an impact on the effectiveness of instruction and the capacity to use innovative teaching strategies.

- **Effects on Community-Based and Nonprofit Training Programs**

Training programs that are community-based and nonprofit may be impacted by economic fluctuations. These programs' ability to offer marginalized communities opportunities for skill development is limited because they frequently rely on funding and donations, which may decline during economic downturns.

- **Student Loan Difficulties**

Economic downturns may make student loan difficulties worse. People may have trouble repaying their loans, which can affect their ability to pursue additional training or education as well as their financial stability.

- **Programs for Study Abroad and Global Mobility**

Study abroad programs and international mobility can be impacted by economic fluctuations. Decreased financial resources might make it harder for students to take part in international learning opportunities, which would limit their exposure to different viewpoints and global skill development.

5. Health Inequalities

In a situation where vulnerable populations face increased health disparities, economic instability directly affects access to healthcare. This section looks into how marginalized communities are disproportionately affected by financial hardships and limited access to health services. The effects go beyond short-term health issues; they also feed the cycle of inequality and poverty.

- **Limited Access to Affordable Healthcare**

Limited resources may make healthcare more expensive for underprivileged populations.

Delays or foregone medical care can have an impact on overall health outcomes, as can higher out-of-pocket expenses, insurance coverage gaps, and restricted access to preventive services.

- **Medical Treatment Obstacles**

Barriers to medical treatment for marginalized communities frequently accompany reduced access to health services. Expenses associated with transportation, a dearth of healthcare facilities in the vicinity, and a shortage of specialists may prevent people from getting the essential medical care.

- **Influence on Health Promotion**

Reduced access to preventive care is partly caused by financial constraints. A higher risk of undiagnosed health conditions and avoidable diseases results from marginalized people's potential financial difficulties in accessing regular check-ups, screenings, and vaccinations.

- **Postponing or Ignoring Medical Procedures**

Financial difficulties may cause essential medical procedures to be postponed or avoided. Because of financial concerns, marginalized communities may put off surgeries or treatments, which can worsen existing conditions and cause new ones.

- **Absence of Health Insurance Protection**

People who live in marginalized communities frequently don't have health insurance. Financial hardships may make it difficult for people to get or keep insurance, which would restrict their access to necessary medical services and raise the cost of those visits.

- **Uneven Mental Health Situations**

Inequalities in mental health are partly caused by financial limitations. Marginalized communities are disproportionately affected by limited access to mental health services, counseling, and therapy, which exacerbates mental health issues and lowers general wellbeing.

- ## Not Enough Resources Arc Available for Chronic Illnesses

People who are marginalized and suffer from chronic illnesses might not have access to enough resources to take care of their health. Financial hardships may make it more difficult to get prescription drugs, medical supplies, and routine monitoring, which increases the risk of developing uncontrolled chronic illnesses.

- ## Effect on the Health of Mothers and Children

The health of mothers and children is disproportionately affected by financial constraints. In underprivileged communities, pregnant people and their unborn children may suffer negative consequences if they have limited access to prenatal care, maternal education, and pediatric services.

- **Restricted Access to Expert Medical Services**

Access to specialized care is frequently impeded by financial limitations. The management of complex health conditions may be impacted by marginalized people's inability to access facilities that offer specialized treatments or to afford the services of specialists.

- **Declines in Program Participation for Health Promotion**

Programs promoting health may see a decline in participation from marginalized populations. Financial limitations can impede participation in wellness, physical activity, and nutrition-focused programs, which can have an impact on preventive measures and general community health.

- **Variations in Dental Wellbeing**

Disparities in dental health are exacerbated by financial limitations. For marginalized people, a lack of access to affordable dental care can lead to untreated dental problems that compromise their oral health and general well-being.

- **Reproductive Health Effects**

Reproductive health disparities are impacted by financial constraints. Reproductive outcomes and family planning choices can be significantly impacted by limited access to family planning services, reproductive healthcare, and fertility treatments, which disproportionately affects people in marginalized communities.

- **A Higher Propensity to Contract Infectious Diseases**

A lack of resources could make people more susceptible to infectious diseases. The risk of outbreaks within marginalized communities can be increased by limited access to vaccinations, healthcare resources, and preventive measures.

- **Restrictions in Health Education Resources**

Resources for health education may be limited as a result of financial constraints. Health literacy and decision-making may be hampered in marginalized communities by difficulties in obtaining information about disease prevention, healthy lifestyles, and available healthcare services.

- **Effects on Social Cohesion**

A decrease in community well-being can be attributed to both financial limitations and restricted access to healthcare services. Inequities can be sustained by a cycle of poverty, low productivity, and systemic issues that arise from health disparities in marginalized communities.

6. Disparities in Housing

By examining how economic instability exacerbates housing disparities, the chapter broadens its focus to include the housing sector. Problems with affordability combined with changes in real estate prices disproportionately affect low-income people and marginalized communities. This section explores the cyclical nature of housing disparities and how economic instability feeds into and perpetuates social disparities by creating unstable living conditions.

- **Effects of Economic Downturns on the Affordability of Housing**

Due to the possibility of job losses or income reductions during downturns, economic instability can exacerbate housing affordability issues. People struggle to make ends meet and pay their rent or mortgages, which exacerbates unstable living conditions.

- **A Higher Chance of Bankruptcies and Evictions**

Foreclosures and evictions are more likely when the economy is unstable. Financially distressed people might find it difficult to fulfill their rental or mortgage payments, which would lead to the loss of homes and exacerbate housing inequality.

- **Difficulty in Finding Affordable Housing**

There may be fewer options for affordable housing during economic downturns. Disparities in housing access may persist as a result of marginalized communities having trouble locating appropriate, reasonably priced homes when housing prices fluctuate.

- **Decreased Funding for Communities with Low Incomes**

Investment in low-income communities may decline as a result of economic instability. Inadequate housing infrastructure, a lack of community resources, and a cycle of social disparities that affect housing conditions can all be caused by this lack of investment.

- **Speculation in the Housing Market and Gentrification**

Economic volatility can lead to gentrification and speculation in the housing market. Opportunities-seeking investors may take advantage of market downturns to purchase real estate, uprooting current residents from underprivileged neighborhoods and worsening housing disparities.

- **Effect on Markets for Rentals**

Rental markets are impacted by economic downturns, which increases competition for reasonably priced apartments. Marginalized people may have to pay more for their rent, have fewer options, and run the risk of being evicted when landlords react to financial pressures.

- **Stress on Dreams of Homeownership**

Ambitions to become homeowners can be strained by economic instability. Disparities in homeownership rates may persist as a result of people and families finding it more difficult to obtain mortgages or amass the required funds.

- **Difficulties Facing Vulnerable Populations**

Economic instability disproportionately affects vulnerable groups, such as marginalized communities and low-income households. Their difficulties in keeping up stable housing conditions make them more vulnerable to homelessness and unstable housing.

- **Effect on Housing Standards**

The standard of housing may be impacted by economic instability. Redevelopment and maintenance projects could be put off or ignored, leading to poor living conditions for people in low-income neighborhoods and escalating social inequalities.

- **Discrimination in Housing and Inequitable Treatment**

Unfair treatment and discrimination in housing can be made worse by economic instability. People who are struggling financially might run into prejudice in the housing market, which would restrict their options and keep social inequities in housing availability alive.

- **Restricted Access to Assistance for Homeownership**

Access to homeownership assistance programs may be restricted during economic downturns. People who are looking for assistance in buying a home, particularly those from underprivileged backgrounds, might encounter a lack of resources, which could make it more difficult for them to end the cycle of housing inequality.

- **Modifying Community Dynamics**

Neighborhood dynamics can change as a result of economic instability. A decline in the economy may exacerbate social inequalities in housing and general well-being by raising crime and decreasing community investment.

- **Strengthening of Racial and Ethnic Divides**

In times of economic instability, racial and ethnic housing disparities are frequently strengthened. Economic difficulties can collide with historical patterns of discrimination, disproportionately affecting minority communities and sustaining inequality.

- **Mortgage and Credit Markets Accessibility**

Access to credit and the mortgage market are impacted by economic volatility. Difficulties in securing advantageous loan conditions could prevent marginalized people from becoming homeowners, which would restrict their options and increase the gap in housing.

- **The Difficulties of Breaking the Pattern**

Individuals and communities find it difficult to break the cycle of housing inequalities because of their cyclical nature. Inclusive communities find it more difficult to attain long-term stability and upward mobility when living conditions are unstable due to economic instability.

Groups at Risk and Social Safety Nets

The chapter explores how economic instability adds to the difficulties faced by vulnerable populations by examining the function of social safety nets. When the economy is struggling, the effectiveness of social assistance programs becomes crucial. The chapter examines how marginalized communities' ability to withstand economic hardships is influenced by the efficiency of safety nets.

- **Social Assistance Program Access**

By giving marginalized communities access to social assistance programs, safety net effectiveness affects their resilience. Strong and easily accessible safety nets, like welfare and unemployment insurance, can provide financial assistance during hard times, enabling people and families to overcome obstacles.

- **Assistance and Protection for Health Care**

Through healthcare coverage and support, effective safety nets increase the resilience of marginalized communities. Programs for accessible healthcare, such as Medicaid or other public health initiatives, guarantee that people can obtain medical care even during uncertain economic times, thereby enhancing their general well-being.

• Programs for Housing Stability

Safety nets are essential for stable housing. Programs that guarantee access to stable housing even in the face of financial difficulties—such as housing assistance, rental subsidies, or support against eviction—help marginalized communities become more resilient.

• Food Security Programs

The impact of safety net effectiveness on marginalized communities' food security is evident. Programs that address immediate needs during economic downturns, such as food assistance, community pantries, and nutrition support, lower the risk of hunger and malnutrition and thus promote resilience.

- **Employment Assistance and Training for Jobs**

The resilience of marginalized communities is increased through safety nets that offer employment assistance and job training. These programs provide opportunities for skill development and job placement, enabling individuals to secure sustainable employment and adjust to changing economic conditions.

- **Opportunities for Education and Learning**

Education and learning opportunities are also part of effective safety nets. The resilience of marginalized communities is enhanced by programs that facilitate access to affordable education, scholarships, and vocational training, which also help people develop the skills necessary for better employment opportunities.

- **Financial Counseling and Debt Relief**

Safety nets that offer financial counseling and debt relief help people become more resilient by tackling personal financial difficulties. These initiatives assist people in handling debt, navigating financial challenges, and establishing a stronger financial foundation.

- **Social Services and Support for the Community**

Social services and community support are good indicators of how well safety nets are working. Enhancing social programs, mental health services, and community networks all help marginalized communities become more resilient by creating a safe haven in times of economic uncertainty.

- **Specialized Support for Vulnerable Populations**

When safety nets in marginalized communities provide targeted support to vulnerable groups, they work best. By addressing systemic disparities, programs designed to meet the unique needs of people who are discriminated against, such as members of racial or ethnic minorities, improve resilience.

- **Safety Net Program's Adaptability and Flexibility**

The ability of safety net programs to be flexible and adaptable affects the resilience of poor communities. Support is kept current and efficient during uncertain times by having systems that can react fast to shifting demands and economic situations.

- **Campaigns for Outreach and Awareness**

The success of safety nets depends on public education and awareness initiatives. By guaranteeing that people are aware of and able to obtain the support they require, programs that actively educate marginalized communities about resources and forms of support improve resilience.

- **Enforcing Rights and Providing Legal Protections**

Safety nets support resilience by upholding rights and offering legal protections. Programs that tackle problems like consumer protection, tenant rights, and workplace discrimination improve the financial stability of underprivileged communities and foster resilience in general.

- **Cooperation with Neighborhood Associations**

Resilience initiatives are strengthened when safety nets and community organizations work together. It is ensured that safety nets are adapted to the particular needs of marginalized communities and that those in need are successfully reached through partnerships with neighborhood nonprofits, advocacy groups, and grassroots organizations.

- **Cutting Down on Systemic Inequalities**

The efficacy of safety nets is intimately linked to initiatives aimed at diminishing systemic disparities. The implementation of policies that target structural obstacles and advance social justice can enhance long-term resilience by addressing the underlying causes of economic hardships encountered by marginalized communities.

- **Ongoing Assessment and Enhancement**

When safety nets are continuously improved and evaluated, marginalized communities become more resilient. Programs are kept responsive, effective, and in line with the changing needs of people and communities dealing with financial difficulties through regular assessments.

Consequences for Policy and Inclusive Growth

The last section of the chapter looks at the implications of policy for addressing social inequality that is made worse by unstable economies. It investigates how social programs, focused interventions, and inclusive economic policies can lessen the effects on marginalized groups. The significance of encouraging inclusive growth in order to build a more just and resilient society is emphasized in this section.

- **Taking Care of Income Inequality**

Addressing income inequality requires promoting inclusive growth. Inclusive growth contributes to a more equitable distribution of wealth and lessens income disparities by guaranteeing that the benefits of the economy are shared more fairly among all societal segments.

- **Encouraging Financial Mobility**

Encouraging inclusive growth is essential for fostering economic mobility. Everyone can advance economically, ending the cycle of poverty and building a more resilient society, when opportunities for education, employment, and entrepreneurship are open to all.

- **Boosting Integration in Society**

Reduced economic gaps between various groups are one way that inclusive growth promotes social cohesion. Enhancing social cohesion and mitigating the likelihood of social instability is possible through fostering a collective sense of prosperity through a fairer allocation of resources and opportunities.

- **Increasing Educational Access**

Access to high-quality education for all is prioritized in inclusive growth. This emphasis guarantees equal learning and skill development opportunities for all people, irrespective of their financial status, thereby promoting a more knowledgeable and resilient community.

- **Assistance for Local and Small Enterprises**

It is important to assist small and local businesses in order to promote inclusive growth. When these businesses prosper, the local economy becomes more resilient overall, diversity of the economy is promoted, and job opportunities are created within the community.

- **Minimizing Underemployment and Unemployment**

By generating a variety of job opportunities, inclusive growth seeks to lower unemployment and underemployment. People are more likely to find fulfilling work when a variety of industries and skill levels are valued, which promotes economic stability on the whole.

- **Increasing the Power of Marginalized Groups**

By lowering obstacles to economic engagement, inclusive growth gives marginalized groups more power. Marginalized communities can actively participate in and profit from the economic development of society as a whole when policies and initiatives address historical inequalities.

- **Developing Infrastructure for All**

Building infrastructure that benefits all societal members is a key component of inclusive growth. Inclusive infrastructure development guarantees that basic services and amenities are accessible to all, promoting societal resilience in everything from healthcare facilities to transportation networks.

- **Promoting Entrepreneurship and Innovation**

Diverse individuals are encouraged to innovate and pursue entrepreneurship through inclusive growth. Societies can access a larger talent pool and foster economic resilience through innovation by supporting innovative ideas and a variety of business endeavors.

- **Increasing Medical Results**

Equality in growth and better health outcomes are related. A healthier and more resilient population that can withstand obstacles related to health is the result of economic development that prioritizes access to healthcare services and supports healthy living conditions.

- **Improving Access to Finance**

Financial inclusion for all societal segments is emphasized by inclusive growth. People can develop financial resilience and engage more actively in the economy by having access to banking, credit, and other financial resources, especially those living in underprivileged areas.

- **Encouraging Sustainability in the Environment**

Promoting environmental sustainability is a necessary part of fostering inclusive growth. An equitable and well-rounded strategy for economic growth takes into account the environment's long-term effects, guaranteeing that growth is resilient and sustainable in the face of ecological difficulties.

- **Minimizing Exposure to Financial Disasters**

One way to lessen vulnerability to economic shocks is through inclusive growth. The economy is more resilient to external shocks when it comprises a diverse range of sectors and income groups, as this helps to evenly distribute the effects of downturns.

- **Boosting the Social Safety Nets**

Growth that is inclusive strengthens social safety nets. Strong social safety programs that offer a safety net for people and communities experiencing financial difficulties are frequently established as a result of policies that promote inclusivity, strengthening society as a whole.

- **Maintaining Long-Term Financial Stability**

In order to guarantee long-term economic stability, inclusive growth must be promoted. Growth that is inclusive is more sustainable because it is based on the involvement and well-being of the whole population, which builds a society that is flexible and resilient.

This chapter, in summary, sheds light on the complex mechanisms through which economic instability exacerbates social inequality. The narrative highlights the pressing need for comprehensive strategies to break the cycle of inequality sustained by economic uncertainties, encompassing wealth disparities as well as unequal access to housing, healthcare, work, education, and employment.

Chapter 9

Coping Strategies and Adaptability

This chapter shows how people can adapt to changing economic conditions by examining the different coping strategies people use. From peer support to individual tactics, it illuminates the human ability to adjust and endure.

1. Budgetary Modifications

Citizens frequently turn to budgetary adjustments as their main means of coping during periods of economic instability. This entails examining and altering spending patterns, reducing expenses that are not necessary, and embracing a more economical approach to money management.

2. Use of Emergency Savings

People can use their emergency funds as a safety net against fluctuations in the economy. This coping strategy provides a short-term financial safety net during hard times by utilizing savings that have already been established to pay for urgent expenses.

3. Increasing the Variety of Income Sources

Diving into different revenue streams is a common strategy for coping with economic volatility. To supplement their primary income and improve their financial resilience, citizens look into alternative revenue streams like part-time jobs, freelancing, or gig economy opportunities.

4. Debt Reduction Techniques

When faced with economic uncertainty, citizens use a variety of debt management techniques. This entails settling debts with creditors, reorganizing payment schedules, and negotiating terms in order to lessen short-term financial strain and prevent long-term issues.

5. Training and Development of Skills

People frequently turn to skill development and education to improve employability and adapt to shifting economic landscapes. This coping strategy entails learning new skills or improving current ones in order to negotiate uncertain economic times and stay competitive in the job market.

6. Networks of Community Support

Coping strategies go beyond personal initiatives and include social support systems in the community. During periods of economic instability, citizens can share resources, information, and emotional support by turning to mutual aid groups, informal lending networks, and community resources.

7. Side Projects and Entrepreneurship

Some people use side businesses or entrepreneurship as a coping technique. In order to create additional revenue streams and promote financial stability outside of traditional employment, this entails launching small businesses, doing freelance work, or commercializing skills.

8. Mental Health Assistance and Psychological Resilience

Having psychological resilience is often necessary to deal with economic instability. People may turn to counseling or therapy as well as other mental health services to help them deal with the stress, anxiety, and uncertainty that come with financial difficulties.

9. Programs for Government Assistance

Government assistance programs can be a vital source of coping for citizens. This entails utilizing unemployment insurance, social safety nets, and other government-funded financial assistance programs to ease financial hardships.

10. Planning for Strategic Savings and Investments

Planning for savings and making wise investments are crucial coping strategies when the economy is unstable. In order to gradually increase financial resilience, this entails making wise investment choices, such as diversifying portfolios, and long-term savings planning.

In conclusion, people use a wide range of coping strategies when faced with unstable economic conditions. People show adaptability and resourcefulness to navigate difficult economic environments in a variety of ways, from skill development, community support, and strategic investments to budgetary adjustments and emergency savings utilization.

Chapter 10

The Path to Restoration

This chapter examines possible avenues for economic recovery as well as steps that can be taken to lessen the effects on the general public. It discusses individual acts, community projects, and policy changes that support the restoration of prosperity and stability.

1. Fiscal Incentives and Public Spending

To boost economic activity, governments can enact fiscal stimulus packages, which involve augmenting public spending on social programs, infrastructure projects, and other related endeavors. This financial infusion has the potential to strengthen companies, generate jobs, and accelerate economic expansion.

2. Monetary Policy Interventions

Monetary policy tools that central banks can use to affect borrowing costs and promote investment include quantitative easing and interest rate adjustments. These steps are intended to promote economic recovery and increase financial system liquidity.

3. Programs for Job Creation

Challenges with unemployment can be directly addressed by putting in place targeted job creation initiatives. To increase employment opportunities, governments should encourage entrepreneurship, invest in industries with room for growth, and offer hiring incentives.

4. Assistance for Small and Medium-Sized Businesses (SMEs)

These engines of economic activity can be strengthened by providing SMEs with financial support, tax breaks, and streamlined regulations. This support fosters entrepreneurship, protects jobs, and builds a more robust and diverse economy.

5. Social Security

For people who are struggling financially, strengthening social safety nets, such as welfare and unemployment benefits can provide a vital lifeline. These steps lessen the negative effects of economic downturns on those who are already at risk.

6. Training and Education Programs

Investing in training and education programs can equip individuals with the skills needed for emerging industries. This proactive approach addresses unemployment by aligning the workforce with evolving economic demands.

7. Infrastructure Investment

Large-scale infrastructure projects not only create immediate job opportunities but also contribute to long-term economic growth. Investments in transportation, energy, and technology infrastructure can enhance a country's competitiveness.

8. **Debt Relief and Restructuring**

Implementing measures for debt relief and restructuring can alleviate the burden on individuals and businesses struggling with debt. This may involve renegotiating loan terms, providing moratoriums, or developing debt reduction programs.

9. **Worldwide Collaboration**

Cooperation with foreign organizations, partners, and neighboring nations can improve economic recovery. A more stable economic environment around the world is facilitated by coordinated policies, cooperative initiatives, and trade agreements.

10. **Support for mental wellness and health**

Understanding how economic instability affects people psychologically, governments and organizations can fund mental health services and wellbeing initiatives. This all-encompassing strategy takes into account the emotional and financial facets of citizens' lives.

11. Adoption of Innovation and Technology

The economy can recover by promoting technological adoption and innovation across industries. This entails promoting digitization projects, research and development, and fostering an atmosphere that encourages technical breakthroughs.

12. All-inclusive Rules

Making inclusive policies a top priority guarantees that everyone in society will profit from the economic recovery. A more equitable recovery is facilitated by initiatives that lessen social inequality, foster diversity, and provide marginalized groups with opportunities.

Combining these policies in a way that is unique to each nation's circumstances can help to lessen the effects on the populace and open the door for economic recovery. The cooperation of corporations, civil society, and the government is often necessary for these routes to be effective.

Conclusion

The unwavering spirit of inventiveness and resilience emerges as an expression of hope for people navigating uncertain times in the face of economic instability. When we consider the difficulties brought about by changes in the economy, it becomes necessary to focus on solutions that enable people and communities to withstand the turbulence caused by uncertain finances.

Building a society that is resilient to economic upheavals requires significant investments in comprehensive healthcare systems, accessible education, and strong social safety nets. Governments and legislators are essential in creating policies that both lessen the effects of economic volatility and create an atmosphere in which people can prosper in the face of hardship.

In addition, fostering a culture of lifelong learning, upskilling, and flexibility is essential to giving people the skills they need to succeed in dynamic job markets. Policies that encourage self-employment, assist small companies, and grant credit can enable people to carve out their own paths during uncertain economic times.

In conclusion, there is potential for proactive problem-solving and group effort rather than a narrative of hopelessness surrounding economic instability. Societies can not only weather economic storms but also emerge stronger, more adaptable, and united in the pursuit of shared prosperity if they cultivate an environment that prioritizes member's well-being and empowerment.

www.ingramcontent.com/pod-product-compliance
Lightning Source LLC
Chambersburg PA
CBHW070922260726
48661CB00003B/790

9 798869 548122